Disclaimer

The publisher of this book is by no way associated with the National Institute of Standards and Technology (NIST). The NIST did not publish this book. It was published by 50 page publications under the public domain license.

50 Page Publications.

Book Title: Autonomy Levels for Unmanned Systems (ALFUS) FrameworkVolume II: Framework Models Initial Version

Book Author: Hui-Min Huang; Elena R. Messina

Book Abstract: This document describes the current Framework models of the overall Autonomy Levels for Unmanned Systems Framework, or ALFUS. ALFUS addresses the autonomy issues along the lifecycle of the unmanned system (UMS), particularly, the autonomy issues at the lifecycle stages of requirements specification, testing and evaluation, and performance measures. ALFUS also augments additional UMS major concerns including safety and risk. ALFUS contains a Metric Model that is composed of metrics along the three established axes or aspects. ALFUS is generic and applicable to multiple UMS domains. This document also discusses how ALFUS might be applied to selected domains that include military, homeland security, and manufacturing. Ongoing issues and future directions are also addressed.

Citation: NIST SP - 1011-II-1.0

Keyword: automony;contextual autonomous capability (CAC);environment;human independence (HI);human robot interaction (HRI)

NIST Special Publication 1011-II-1.0

AUTONOMY LEVELS FOR UNMANNED SYSTEMS (ALFUS) FRAMEWORK

Volume II: Framework Models
Version 1.0

Contributed by the Ad Hoc ALFUS Working Group Participants[1]

Sponsored by:

Hui-Min Huang

Elena Messina

James Albus, Ph.D.

December 2007

---

[1] See CONTRIBUTORS list.

DEDICATION

Mom, I know that you would smile to see this report. I was typing it at your bedside during your final days, while you were reminiscing about the old, old hometown.

You and Dad have held everyone in the family so deeply together, weathering storm after storm. You gave us all you have, yet never asked anything for yourself. Even in the last day when I had to leave, you comforted me.

I will forever treasure those days being together with you.

Hui-Min

June 11, 2007

CONTENTS

FIGURES

CONTRIBUTORS

The following list contains practitioners who have been contributing to the ALFUS effort through Workshop discussions, document review, and email correspondences offering field experiences. Those who, at various stages of the effort, have been instrumental to particular aspects of the ALFUS Framework are highlighted in SEGMENT I of the list and the rest of the contributors are included in SEGMENT II.

We apologize if any contributors have been omitted or misplaced. Please inform us to get the list updated. Contractors are acknowledged by the organizations or programs that they support. As the development effort rolls on, the list is anticipated to be reorganized per the evolution of the Framework.

The funding sources are acknowledged at the end of this list.

Organizational acronyms for the contributors are provided first in the following:

AATD	Aviation Applied Technology Directorate
AFRL	Air Force Research Laboratory
AMRDEC	Aviation and Missile Research, Development and Engineering Center
ARL	Army Research Laboratory
CERDEC	Communications-Electronics Research, Development, and Engineering Center
DARPA	Defense Advanced Research Project Agency
DOC	Department of Commerce
DOD	Department of Defense
DOE	Department of Energy
DOT	Department of Transportation
FCS	Future Combat System
FHWA	Federal Highway Administration
GDRS	General Dynamics Robotics Systems
IDA	Institute for Defense Analysis
INL	Idaho National Laboratory
IPT	Integrated Product Team
JAUS	Joint Architecture for Unmanned Systems
LSI	Lead System Integrator
NAVAIR	Naval Air Systems Command
NDGI	Navigator Development Group, Inc.
NIST	National Institute of Standards and Technology
NRL	Naval Research Laboratory
NSWC	Naval Surface Weapon Center
ONR	Office of Naval Research
OSD	Office of the Secretary, DOD
OUSD	Office of the Under Secretary, DOD
SAE	Society of Automotive Engineers

SSEI	System of Systems Engineering and Integration
SWRI	Southwest Research Institute
TACOM	Tank-Automotive Command
TARDEC	TACOM Research, Development and Engineering Center
TRADOC	Training and Doctrine Command
UAMBL	Unit of Action Maneuver Battle Laboratory
UGV	Unmanned Ground Vehicle
USSCOM	U.S. Special Operations Command

SEGMENT I:

Kerry Pavek
L3 Communications
U.S. Army TRADOC Command
Capabilities Manager, FCS

Eric Hansen
U.S. Navy NSWC

Salvatore P. Schipani, Ph.D.
U.S. DOC, NIST

Mark Ragon
The Boeing Company
U.S. Army FCS LSI SSEI IPT

Jeffry Jones
NDGI
U.S. Army FCS LSI SSEI IPT

Robert Smith
U.S. AFRL

Keith Arthur
U.S. Army AATD

Raymond Higgins
U.S. Army AATD

Robert Wade
U.S. Army AMRDEC

Woody English
DeVivo AST, Inc.
Chair, SAE AS-4 Committee

Brian Novak
U.S. Army TARDEC

David Bruemmer
U.S. DOE INL

Charles Bishop
The Boeing Company
U.S. Army FCS LSI UGV IPT

Anthony Barbera, Ph.D.
U.S. DOC, NIST

SEGMENT II (in alphabetical order):

Adams, Curt—U.S. Army TACOM/ U.S. Army FCS
Adams, Thomas— The Boeing Company, FCS LSI
Altshuler, Thomas—Rockwell Scientific Company
Anderson, Keith—U.S. DOD
Antonishek, Brian—NIST
Barnhill, Robert MAJ—U.S. Army
Bergman, John—FCS Support
Brayman, Darryl—AFRL Support
Brendle, Bruce—U.S. Army TACOM
Cagle-West, Marsha—U.S. Army AMRDEC
Cerny, Jeffrey—U.S. Army AMRDEC
Clough, Bruce—U.S. Air Force AFRL
Connelly, Julianna—IDA
Dzugan, Michael—U.S. Army CERDEC
Ferlis, Robert—U.S. DOT FHWA
Fleck, Dale—Lockheed Martin Company
Gage, Douglas—DARPA/XPM Technologies
Gage, Gerrie LTC—DARPA
Hart, Jeremy--NASA
Hill, Susan G.—U.S. Army, ARL
Hirtz, Julie—U.S. Army
Hodge, Kelley A. MAJ—U.S. Army
Huang, Peter—U.S. DOT FHWA
Juberts, Maris—NIST
Kania, Robert—U.S. Army TACOM
Klarquist, William —Perceptek Robotics Company, FCS Support
Knichel, David— U.S. Army Maneuver Support Center
Kotora, Jeffrey— Chairman, JAUS Working Group, OSD Support (L3)
Laflamme, Mark—U.S. Army

Maijala, Brian K—U.S. Army
Mamplata, Caesar G.—U.S. Navy NAVAIR
Mayhew, Gregory—Boeing Company, FCS LSI
McWilliams, George—SWRI
Melick, Peter—U.S. Army
Moorthy, Jay—U.S. Army AATD
Nardi, Gregory J—U.S. Army UAMBL
Nielson, Curtis—U.S. INL
Overstreet, Dennis—DARPA Support (SRS Tech)
Pena, Richard—FCS Support
Peot, Mark—Rockwell Scientific Company
Pusey, Jason—U.S. Army
Rolader, G.—SAIC Company, FCS LSI
Rovegno, John COL—U.S. Army
Rodgers, Dan—GDRS Company, FCS
Scholtz, Jean—NIST (retired)
Schultz, Alan C.—U.S. Navy NRL
Scott, Harry—NIST
Shoemaker, Charles— U.S. Army ARL (retired)
Sparrow, David—IDA
Steinberg, Marc—U.S. Navy ONR
Swan, Stephen—DOD Support
Tasker, Chirag R.— SAIC Company, FCS LSI
Wade, Robert—U.S. AMRDEC
Walther, Robert—USSOCOM
Wavering, Albert—NIST
Weber, Thomas— U.S. DOE
Wit, Jeffrey— U.S. Air Force AFRL Support

Funding support for the ALFUS effort has been provided by:

U. S. Department of Commerce
    National Institute of Standards and Technology

Department of Homeland Security
    Science and Technology Directorate
    Standards Executive
    Sponsor: Dr. Bert Coursey

The U.S. ARL provided partial funding support at the early stage of the effort.

FORWARD

The Autonomy Levels for Unmanned Systems (ALFUS) Ad Hoc Workgroup is a National Institute of Standards and Technology (NIST) sponsored effort and is participated by Government Labs, developers, users, and contractors of various Unmanned Systems (UMS) programs. The participants have formed close collaborative relationships, including the U.S. Army Future Combat System (FCS) User community and the Lead System Integrator (LSI) and its contractors.

ALFUS aims at formulating, through a consensus-based approach, a logical framework for characterizing the UMS autonomy, covering issues of levels of autonomy, mission complexity, and environmental complexity. The Framework is to provide standard definitions, metrics, and process for the specification, evaluation, and development of the autonomous capabilities of UMSs. The Framework is also intended to facilitate communication among the practitioners.

ALFUS is an ongoing project. At the 16th Workshop, held in April 2007, it was decided that the results should be published as the initial version of the ALFUS Framework while the development effort continues. As such, this document serves the purposes of both describing the current results as well as identifying issues and future directions. This document also reflects the evolutionary notion of the Framework. For example, the central concept for ALFUS was originally called levels of autonomy (LOA) or autonomy levels but was eventually renamed as Contextual Autonomous Capability (CAC).

Readers are encouraged to contribute to the ALFUS effort by means of reviewing and commenting the metrics and process, participating in the quarterly Workshops, and experimenting with the metrics and forwarding us the comments and suggestions. The web site: http://www.isd.mel.nist.gov/projects/autonomy_levels/ provides the ALFUS project information. Correspondences can be forwarded to:

Hui-Min Huang
Intelligent System Division
National Institute of Standards and Technology
100 Bureau Drive, Mail Stop 8230
Gaithersburg, MD 20899
Tel: 301 975-3427
Email: hui-min.huang@nist.gov
http://www.isd.cme.nist.gov/personnel/huang/index.htm

1   INTRODUCTION

Since the inception of the ALFUS[2] concept and the Ad Hoc Workgroup, in 2003, 17 ALFUS workshops have been conducted. This document describes the results of the ALFUS framework models as of December 2007.

In the inaugural Workshop, held at NIST, UMS practitioners from more than 20 Government organizations, both military and civilian, presented their perspectives, covering unmanned aerial systems or vehicle (UAS or UAV)s, unmanned ground vehicle (UGV)s, unmanned surface vehicle (USV)s, and unmanned underwater vehicle (UUV)s. They described how an anticipated ALFUS framework might facilitate their particular programs, which aspects of the programs are to be measured using ALFUS, the current metrics that they were employing, etc. Common understanding and requirements for ALFUS were derived from the presentations to form the starting point for the ALFUS framework. See Appendix B for descriptions on the ALFUS historical background.

Although it is well recognized that interests and needs in ALFUS extended widely in the UMS community, the inaugural workshop participants resolved that the participation at the early stage of the ALFUS development effort should be limited to a core group of government participants, including their representing contractors. The purposes were to expediently establish:

- the feasibility of the ALFUS concept
- the critical mass on the core issues and knowledge, particularly focusing on a generic, National level scope
- the collaborating use cases
- the workshop approach and operating model and the path for the eventual open participation.

The accomplishments for this early stage were highlighted with the publication of the ALFUS Terminology document [1]. It has begun to be adopted, referenced, or otherwise used in other standards and public documents, including the ASTM International [2] Standards E2521-07 and F 2541-06 for various UMSs, Unmanned Systems Safety Guide for DoD Acquisition [3], Joint Architecture for Unmanned Systems (JAUS) [4, 5], performance measures for the urban search and rescue (US&R) robots for a Department of Homeland Security (DHS) program [6], and other public documents such as [7]. Many requests for copies as well as invitations for seminars from various organizations have also been furnished.

The early stage accomplishments also include the establishment of the three-axis conceptual model for the ALFUS framework and the some of the key concepts for the metrics sets. We also resolved to strive for technical flexibility in order to maximize the workshop productivity.

---

[2] [1] also provides a comprehensive list of ALFUS related acronyms.

Once the objectives for the early stage were achieved, the ALFUS workshops entered their second phase, in 2004, by inviting the identified collaborating project team, the U.S. Army FCS program LSI and associated contractors to the meetings. FCS was selected because, at that time, the program involved the largest DOD family of robotic systems anticipated to use increasing levels of autonomy. Also, the program was at a stage of systems engineering requiring the same types of autonomy definitions that the ALFUS Workgroup was addressing.

Subsequently, the participants determined that the Workshops would be open to the general UMS community.

1.1 Organization of the Document

Section 1 describes the objectives, discusses the requirements, and states the rationale for the ALFUS framework. The overall concepts of the framework follow, in Section 2. Sections 3 through 5 describe the three sets of metrics. Characteristics and issues for the metrics are described in Section 6. These metrics are further formulated to form ALFUS level models and the associated processes, as described in Sections 7 and 8. Sections 9 and 10 cover application, benefits, and future directional issues. A summary is given in Section 11. Readers with different levels of familiarity with the Framework or with different types of needs might choose to read the particular sections that are most suitable. For example, the levels of human interaction might be the main concern for a particular program.

1.2 The Need: Metrics and Definitions

Robotic autonomy technology has matured enough for UMSs to be deployed to assist military and civilian operations in a wide range of application areas, such as Defense [8, 9, 10], US&R operations [11, 12, 13, 14], border surveillance [15, 16, 17], Explosive Ordnance Disposal (EOD) [18, 19, 20], intelligent transportation systems [21], space exploration [22, 23, 24], and medical and service applications [25, 26, 27, 28]. A particular and important issue for UMSs, the performance metrics, has been undertaken by NIST [29, 30, 31].

UMSs vary widely in their capabilities and purposes. They may be developed either with particular requirements or for general purposes. Some of the operating environments may be well structured and the UMSs are tasked to perform repetitive but unsupervised tasks. Other environments may be much more unpredictable which require the UMSs to make spontaneous decisions based on the perceived environmental conditions through onboard sensing and processing capabilities. The problem space needs to be thoroughly analyzed, in detail, so that UMS solutions can be effectively and efficiently devised.

These topics point to the requirement of a comprehensive, standard framework that allows practitioners to communicate on the operational and development issues, to analyze the mission requirements, and to evaluate the capabilities of the UMSs. The ALFUS framework is, therefore, so conceived. In developing this Framework, the Workgroup intends to review or leverage existent concepts and results as developed by other organizations or researchers, including the U.S. DOD Joint Ground Robotics Enterprise (JGRE) [32], U.S. Air Force and Army [33, 34, 35, 36], the U.S. Department of Transportation [37], National Aeronautics and

Space Administration (NASA) [38], academia [39, 40, 41, 42], as well as relevant results from areas of machine intelligence [43], human-robot interaction (HRI) [44, 45, 46, 47, 4849, 50], etc.

Throughout the 17 Workshops, a vast amount of technical issues pertaining to ALFUS has been resolved. The results were published in various venues [51, 52, 53, 54, 55, 56, 57]. This Framework document summarizes the latest results, identifies the issues to be resolved, as well as provides guidelines on how the Framework might be used.

1.3   ALFUS Objectives

The overall objectives for ALFUS are:

- Standard terms and definitions for characterizing the autonomous capability for unmanned systems.
- Metrics, processes, and tools for facilitating measuring and evaluating the autonomy of unmanned systems.

By establishing common terms and metrics, emerging robotic technologies can be analyzed, compared, and assessed in a formal and methodical manner.

1.4   ALFUS Approach

- Metrics based.
- Multiple layers of abstraction for autonomy requirements and capabilities.
- Extendable to general performance metrics model for UMSs.

1.5   ALFUS Scope

- Generic framework covering all UMSs.
- From remote control through full and intelligent autonomy.
- From single UMS, low level operational behavior to joint missions.
- Application domains include, but are not limited to military, manufacturing, logistics, search and rescue, service, medical, and elder and handicap assist.

1.6   ALFUS Additional Potential Benefits

The benefits of ALFUS could extend beyond the main objectives into the following:

1.6.1 Enhance Safety

Human safety is of the utmost concern in the modern society. However, in such a society, there are more and more tasks not suited for humans. Particularly, there are tasks that must be performed in environments that may be:

- dangerous—where heavy machinery may be operating, a building may be collapsing, or chemical, biological, radioactive, nuclear, and explosive material might be emitted

- extreme—where it may be too hot, too cold, or too confined

- hostile—where one may come under enemy fire.

In a hostile environment, certain skills and certain workload levels may be required from the operator at certain portions of the mission. The difficulty of the assigned tasks may not exceed certain levels. These are just some examples for ALFUS application. ALFUS also facilitates formal and quantitative measures that would ease testing and evaluation. These features, in turn, augment safety engineering for UMS.

1.6.2 Improve UMS Performance and Enhance Outcome

It has been well recognized that there are tasks suited for autonomous systems, including those repetitive and boring to humans and those beyond human physical abilities. In other words, by enhancing outcome, we mean for the UMS to achieve:

- mission/task/order goals

- accuracy, in time and space

- repeatability

- savings in time, space, and material

Those environments and tasks must be characterized so that appropriately equipped UMSs can be developed and deployed. A UMS with high acting/executing capability has a better chance of achieving a task requiring high precision. ALFUS is attempted to facilitate these purposes.

UMSs must be fully understood and characterized in terms of their autonomous capabilities in order to maximize their potentials and generate these benefits. ALFUS is intended to provide a toolset to facilitate this characterization and exploration process.

2 METRIC FRAMEWORK

The framework describes the core knowledge, including definitions, metrics, and processes and guidelines that supports the specification, analysis, and characterization of UMS autonomous capability.

2.1 Key Definitions

Key definitions were generated in the ALFUS effort to serve as the basis for further Framework development.

A. Unmanned System (UMS)

"A powered physical system, with no human operator aboard the principal components, acts on physical world for the purpose of achieving assigned tasks. May be mobile or stationary. May include any and all associated supporting components. Examples include unmanned ground vehicles (UGV), unmanned aerial vehicles (UAV), unmanned underwater vehicles (UUV), unmanned water surface borne vehicles (USV), unattended munitions (UM), and unattended ground sensors (UGS). Missiles, rockets, and their submunitions, and artillery are not considered UMSs."

The first issue regarding the definition is, what is/are the minimum requirement(s) to be a UMS. The first tier requirement may be a robotic vehicle without a human onboard. This robotic vehicle is the main entity in the UMS that receives and acts on the defined goals.

The second tier requirement may be regarding HRI. If the HRI devices exist and are integral parts of the functionality of the robotic vehicles, i.e., when these entities are needed for the goals, they are parts of the UMSs. In various application domains the HRI device may be called an Operator Control Unit (OCU) or a Ground Control Station (GCS). Ultimately, the goals assigned to UMS come from the HRI.

The third tier requirement may be whether the other associated manned or unmanned subsystems are integral parts of the functionality of the robotic vehicles. In other words, when these entities are needed for achieving the goals, then they are parts of the UMS. However, they must serve the supportive roles within the context of achieving the goals.

Note that the supportive, manned subsystems might dominate in sheer physical sizes or in terms of the portion of the processing that they provide. The whole integral system should still be called a UMS. Similarly, when a hybrid or dual-use vehicle operates in the unmanned manner, it is considered a UMS, but not when it operates under manned control.

These point out that, in some situations, a robotic vehicle may be developed to be solely unmanned and is always considered a UMS, whereas in some other situations, a robotic vehicle may or may not be considered a UMS depending on how it is deployed and what assignments it is performing.

B. Autonomy

"A UMS's own ability of integrated sensing, perceiving, analyzing, communicating, planning, decision-making, and acting/executing, to achieve its goals as assigned [1]"

We further define the stated, integrated "sensing, perceiving, analyzing, communicating, planning, decision-making, and acting/executing" as **Root Autonomous Capabilities (RACs)**. Note that the essence of "UMS's own ability" is independent of human interactions.

There are also discussions on whether the aspects of learning and world modeling should also be parts of the RACs. They should be resolved in the future workshops and may result in updates to the definition.

C.   Contextual Autonomous Capability (CAC) Model for Unmanned Systems

"A UMS's CAC is characterized by the missions that the system is capable of performing, the environments within which the missions are performed, and human independence that can be allowed in the performance of the missions.

Each of the aspects, or axes, namely, mission complexity (MC), environmental complexity (EC), and human independence (HI) is further attributed with a set of metrics to facilitate the specification, analysis, evaluation, and measurement of the CAC of particular UMSs.

This CAC model facilitates the characterization of UMSs from the perspectives of requirements, capability, and levels of difficulty, complexity, or sophistication. The model also provides ways to characterize UMS's autonomous operating modes. The three axes can also be applied independently to assess the levels of MC, EC, and HI for a UMS."

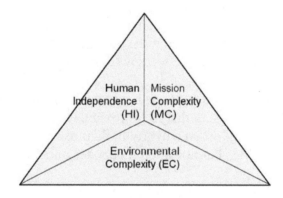

Figure 1: The Three Aspects for ALFUS

The three aspects are depicted in Figure 1. The CAC encompasses the following layers of abstraction:

- At the low layers, a UMS is characterized by the metric scores, including the percentage of a mission that is planned and executed by the UMS onboard processors, the levels of task decomposition, how easy it is to find a solution in the operating environment, etc.

17

- Above the metric layer, a UMS is characterized by the three scores for the aspects or axes, namely, MC, EC, and HI. These axis scores are weighted averages of the individual metric scores.

Key Definitions	Autonomy, Unmanned System (UMS)		
	Contextual Autonomy Capability (CAC)		
Axes / Aspects	Mission Complexity (MC)	Environmental Complexity (EC)	Human Independence (HI) or Level of Autonomy (LOA)
Metrics			
Scales			

Figure 2: ALFUS Tabular Construct

As shown in Figure 2, in ALFUS, the definition for autonomy provides the basis for CAC, which, in turns, provides the basis for the metrics. Note that ALFUS allows for additional layers of details below the metrics layer. For example, the metric of human interaction time along the HI axis might be further decomposed to actuation time, monitoring time, sensory data acquisition time, etc. Further investigation of this issue is planned. A weighted average of the three axis scores to form a single index is also possible, although it is probably an over-simplified index to convey the autonomous capability.

The higher layers facilitate requirements specification and communication purposes, whereas the lower levels facilitate implementation and testing and evaluation.

Conventionally, the notion of autonomy addresses only the human interaction aspect. The reason for the three-aspect model in ALFUS can be illustrated with the following example: a washing machine is not considered to have a high autonomy level just because it does not require human interaction during a wash cycle. Rather, what should concern the practitioners are the overall autonomous requirements or capabilities of the UMS. The Work Group has also been using a three-axis depiction, as shown in Figure 3 to highlight this issue.

Details and additional characteristics of the CAC will be described in the later sections.

Figure 3: The Three-Axis Model for ALFUS

D.   Level of Autonomy (LOA) or Autonomy Level (AL)

"A set of progressive indices, typically given in numbers and/or names, identifying a UMS's capability of performing assigned autonomous missions [1]"

The autonomy level in ALFUS CAC model refers to the HI aspect or axis, with the other two axes providing the context. The relative levels of HI can be determined in the Framework as depicted in Figure 2. Later sections of the document will describe the methods. Note that the term autonomy level is used in different contexts in the research community. Bruemmer, D.J., et al, in [58], uses the term dynamic autonomy. Barynov and Hexmoor used the terms including preference autonomy, choice autonomy, and decision autonomy [39]. All of these are consistent with and can be facilitated by the ALFUS CAC model.

The level may be used in a nominal sense while the instantaneous values may be dynamic or adjusting, to the extent of the system design, along the course of mission execution depending on the changes in the environmental and operating conditions.

Differentiations among consecutive LOAs may or may not be constant. There may even be certain degrees of subjectivity. Therefore, it might be suitable to consider autonomy as a gradual property related to the degree of intervention [59]. This may also be considered *situation-adaptive* as agents (human versus robot) may be assigned control over different parts of a single system simultaneously [60, 61, 62], thus become collaborative [63, 64, 65].

E.   High, Mid, and Low Degrees of CAC

The Framework defines the following three CACs to provide a general reference for further CAC investigation:

- Highest CAC

19

Completes all assigned missions with highest complexity; understands, adapts to, and maximizes benefit/value/efficiency while minimizing costs/risks on the broadest scope environmental and operational changes; capable of total independence from operator intervention.

- Mid CAC

Plans and executes tasks to complete an operator specified mission; limited understanding and response to environmental and operational changes and information; limited ability to reduce costs/risks while increase benefit/value/efficiency; relies on about 50 % operator input

- Lowest CAC

Remote control for simple tasks in simple environment

These concepts can be further illustrated in Figure 4. At the leftmost indication, a UMS may operate at the lowest CAC when the UMS performs a simplest mission using HRI 100 % of the time in a simplest environment. The general trend may be that CAC increases when the levels of HI, MC, and EC increase, as shown from the left to right in the chart.

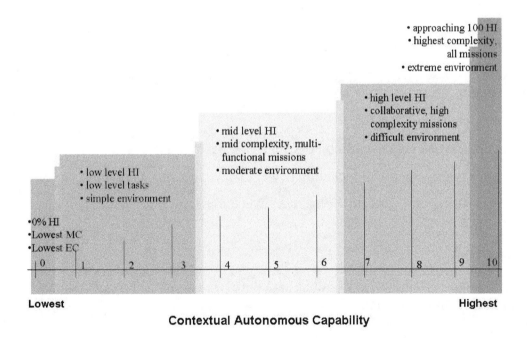

Figure 4: Illustration of CAC

F.   Mode of UMS Operation or UMS Operational Mode

"Human operator's ability to interact with a UMS to perform the operator assigned missions. The following are the defined modes of operation: fully autonomous, semi-autonomous, teleoperation, and remote control."

A distinction exists between autonomy levels and these modes.

2.2   Key Concepts

The CAC definition invited the following questions:

o   What makes a mission complex?

o   What makes an environment complex?

o   What makes a UMS human-independent?

These questions needed to be thoroughly understood before the metrics could be developed. We list our current understanding in the following three subsections. Note that, due to the U.S. Army Future Combat System (FCS) focus of the initial ALFUS work, the mission and the environmental considerations emphasize military situations. Clearly other applications will have considerations specific to their situations.

2.2.1.   What Makes a Mission Complex

- mission time constraint
- precision constraints and repeatability, in navigation, manipulation, detection, perception, etc.
- level of collaboration required
- concurrence and synchronization of events and behaviors
- resource management, for including power, bandwidth, and ammunition
- authority hierarchy, for data access, plan execution, etc.
- rules of engagement
- adversaries
- risks, and survivability; for example, signature reduction of self might add to the complexity of the mission
- knowledge requirements
  - o   knowledge dependence—types and amounts of information required correlate to mission complexity
  - o   a priori knowledge might make planning easier

- o knowledge availability, uncertainty, or learning requirement might make the mission more complex
- o the difficulty in prediction could affect mission complexity

- sensory and the processing requirements
- HI requirements could affect mission planning and execution, thus affecting mission complexity

2.2.2. What Makes an Environment More Complex?

- energy signals, including
  - o acoustic, affecting sensing
  - o Electromagnetic interference (EMI, also called radio frequency interference or RFI), affecting communication, control, and sensors
- absolute and fiducial (reference points) positioning aides, placement of them, global positioning systems (GPS), markers, etc., can facilitate navigation and reduce the complexity
- dynamic nature
  - o stigmergy—environmental effects that were caused by own actions
  - o changes in the surroundings that were not caused by own actions
- object size, type, density, and intent; including natural or man made
- fauna and flora, animal and plant lives in regions of interest, respectively
- hazards, including Chemical, Biological, Radiological/Nuclear, and Explosive (CBRNE), fire, etc.
- meteorological data, affecting visibility and traversability
- light
- terrain
  - o hydrology
  - o sea state
  - o positive (hill, bushes) or negative (cave, ditch) features [1]
- engineered structures
  - o inside, outside
  - o buildings, bridges, tunnels, trenches, wall, fence, power poles/lines

2.2.3.   What Makes a UMS Human Independent

The more a UMS is able to sense, perceive, analyze, communicate, plan, make decisions, and act, the more independent it is. However, it remains an open issue on how to measure the abilities. For example:

- when more of the concerned environmental phenomena can be sensed by the UMS

- when a wider area of concern can be sensed by the UMS

- when the UMS is able to understand and analyze more of the perceived situations

- when a larger portion of the mission plan is generated by the UMS

- when the UMS is able to generate high-level, complex plans as opposed to low-level, straightforward plans

- when the UMS is able to communicate to the right parties with the right information

2.3   Framework Outline

We envision a construct within which a generic framework may be instantiated for program specific ALFUS frameworks. Such a generic framework includes the following components:

1. Terms and Definitions: The first requirement for the Framework that the Ad Hoc Workgroup identified was a set of standard terms and definitions. The published Volume 1 of the ALFUS Framework [1] contains the results. As shown in section 2.1, certain term definitions are keys to the Framework development, either generic or application specific extensions.

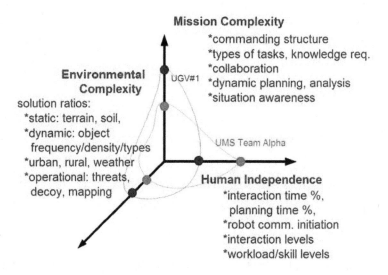

Figure 5: ALFUS Framework Concept

23

2. The Metric model: The construct is defined in Section 2.1. Figure 5 provides a three-axis view that emphasizes the aspects that are critical for dealing with UMS autonomy.

3. The Executive Model: The level of HI (or LOA), level of MC, and level of EC models are defined along the HI, MC, and EC axes, respectively. The latter two models provide context for the LOA model. This is the definition-based aspect of ALFUS. The three models are developed through either the summaries of the metrics, shown in the lower part of Figure 2, or the key definitions, shown in the upper part of the figure.

4. Guidelines, Processes, and Use Cases: These are for applying the generic framework to specific ALFUS applications. Figure 6 illustrates how various types of ALFUS information may be applied at various stages of a UMS lifecycle. Figure 7 illustrates the distinctions between the generic model and the program specific model of ALFUS.

Later sections in this document elaborate these aspects of the Framework.

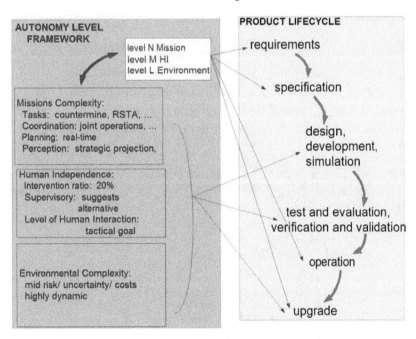

Figure 6: lifecycle Support in ALFUS

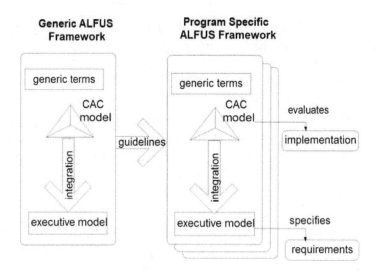

Figure 7: Generic Nature of ALFUS

2.4 ALFUS Models for UMS Safety, Risk and Mission Success

We postulate the following concepts for the applicability of ALFUS:

> *The level of risk for a UMS to perform a mission can be positively corresponding to or proportional to the difference between the requirements and the UMS's possession of CAC. The discrepancies can be along any or all of the three aspects.*

> *When the UMS CAC is equal to or higher than the required levels, lowered risk can be anticipated, although risk may exist even when all the requirements are all fulfilled.*

> *The ALFUS CAC model also augments the analysis of UMS safety. Level of safety may be contributed by the following:*

> o *insufficient capability in any of the RACs [1]*

> o *insufficient scores in any of the metrics/axes, i.e., level of safety can be inversely proportionally to the level of risk*

Safety could also be considered as a subset of complexity, either mission or environmental. Further investigation in this area is needed.

2.5 Generic Nature

Figure 7 illustrates the components and their relationships within ALFUS. Note that the program specific executive models, generated from the generic executive model, are typically used for specifying requirements at the early stages of the product lifecycles, whereas the CAC models are typically used for evaluating the implementations at late stages of the lifecycles.

The guidelines and processes are described, in details in Section 6.7. There are several methods being explored: directly applying the metrics, analyzing autonomy through its definition, and filtering task/mission complexity by filtering up the autonomy from the performance or autonomy basic skills.

3 THE MISSION COMPLEXITY (MC) AXIS/ASPECT

Four groups of metrics are devised to characterize the complexity of missions.

3.1 Tactical Behavior and Tasking Group

- Levels of Task Decomposition

  o Description: How are missions or high-level tasks decomposed into lower level tasks, including basic skills? What is the width and depth of task decomposition for a mission?

  o Scale/Measure: Numbers of levels and of subtasks and skills. Two models can be used:

    A full-scale decomposition of a military mission could include the following levels: division, brigade, battalion, company, platoon, vehicle, skills, primitive, and actuator. There could be even higher levels. Multiple types of UMSs could be involved to conduct joint missions at these high levels. Figure 8 illustrates the point [66]. A detailed discussion of this issue is presented at a later section.

    A simplified task decomposition model considers only three levels, namely, group tasks, vehicle tasks, and skills. In this model, the tasks that are at levels lower than skills implicitly affect the degrees of complexity of the corresponding skills. A similar argument can also be made for the high-level tasks.

- Type of Tasks

  o Description: From mission level groupings of high risk, highly complex tasks to low level, single function tasks.

  o Scale/Measure:

    number of functions involved—C4 (Command and Control, Communications, Computers), Lethality, Survivability, Tactical Behavior, ISR (Intelligence, Surveillance, and Reconnaissance)

    number of UMSs involved

    number of subtasks or skills needed

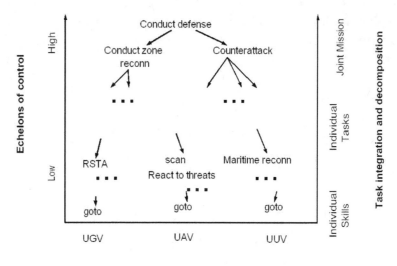

Figure 8: Task Decomposition and Integration

- Complexity of Tasks

  o Description: ability to handle tasking uncertainty (for example, environmental understandability, an EC metric, could contribute to uncertainty in task planning and execution), over vs. under constrained, spatial and temporal precision, information requirements

  o Scale/Measure:

    knowledge requirements--number of knowledge types and associated confidence levels, such as signal, entity, event, image, map, logic, physics, and cultural value

    temporal and spatial resolutions for task execution

    safety and risk levels

    rates of changes of tasks and/or their goals

- Decision Space Structure

  o Description: number of decisions/choices and their couplings

  o Scale/Measure:

    transition/state numbers and ratios, depth/breath of search tree

    rules of engagement

    number of concurrent tasks

This group indicates that multiple factors can be used to identify complexity. For example, a high level mission involving a large team of teams tends to be complex. However, a task for a single vehicle that requires very rich knowledge or involves very high uncertainty may also be complex. Examples include negotiating busy traffic or identifying a person in a large city.

3.2 Collaboration Group

- Agent perspective

  - Description: the level(s) of the mission/task/commanding structure at which collaborations take place, the temporal/spatial/logical location at which collaborations take place

  - Scale/Measure:

    high - mission level collaboration and parenthetical understanding of mission intent;

    medium - collaboration within subsystems, multi-point external collaboration, collaboration at the mission level;

    low - collaboration within subsystems;

    lowest - no collaboration

- Interface/Data Sharing perspective

  - Description: sharing of the data among the subsystems or the components of the unmanned system

  - Scale/Measure: number of channels, types of data, frequencies of exchanges, synchronous/asynchronous

3.3 Planning and Analysis Group

- Dynamic planning

  - Description: UMS's ability to handle mission variations and to perform real-time planning

  - Scale/Measure: degrees of mission variations that the UMS can handle; percentage of mission that can be performed without preplan; effectiveness and efficiency of the planning against operator-generated plans

- Analysis

  - Description: capability of values/cost and benefit/risk analyses

  - Scale/Measure: resulting values and costs, such as fuel savings, amount of intelligence gathered

  - Note: might overlap with some of the Environmental metrics.

3.4 Situation Awareness Group

- Situation awareness

  o Description: situation awareness with respect to the mission intent and environmental understanding

  o Scale/Measure:

    level of spatial scope: strategic, tactic, UMS internal

    level of temporal scope: projection into future, comprehension of current and past situations, perception of current and past situations.

4 THE HUMAN INDEPENDENCE (HI) AXIS/ASPECT

The HI metrics include:

- UMS to Operator Communications or Robotic Initiation

  o Description: the ability for the UMS to identify and communicate and/or negotiate with humans and/or other entities.

  o Scale/Measure: From highest to lowest:

    identifies and negotiates with appropriate individuals,

    initiates appropriate communications with the correct individual,

    initiates appropriate communications with operator,

    operator approval query,

    prioritizes information,

    offers a complete set of information/decision/action alternatives,

    relies on humans to decide what to communicate.

- Ratio of Human Intervention Time / Mission Time

  o Description: the portion of the time during which operators are interacting with the UMS.

    Under conditions of mixed-initiative collaboration [67, 68], required by systems necessitating multi-agent interactions [69, 70], this might be described and measured as *neglect tolerance* [71].

  o Scale/Measure: linear scale from approaching 0 % through 100 %.

- Ratio of Human Planning Time / Mission Time

- o Description: the portion of the mission plan that is pre-generated by human
- o Scale/Measure: linear, numeric percentage

- Level of Human Interaction

  - o Description: the level of authority at which the operator interacts with the UMS
  - o Scale/Measure: From high to low:

        assign mission,

        assign strategic goals,

        assign tactical goals,

        assign mission tasks,

        route,

        auto pilot,

        servo.

- Level of Human Workload

  There are known and accepted methodologies, some with metrics, for assessing operator workload that the ALFUS group must explore. Guidance can be seen in [72, 73]. Aside from physiological measures [74, 75, 76, 77], the concept of mental workload for both primary and secondary task performance should be considered [78, 79], as well as the subjective experience.

  Workload can also be affected depending on how tasks are modeled or defined. Research results include performance moderator functions which attempt to describe the impact of human performance to internal and external stressors [80, 81, 82, 83, 84, 85].

  Note that workload evaluation can be highly subjective. Different evaluators can see different aspects. The evaluation can also greatly depend on attributes such as training, experience, physical conditioning, etc.

- Identified metric candidates

  Sheridan T.B. and his colleagues' work regarding levels of human interaction with automation [39, 41] have been proposed as a metric called robotic independence. Further investigation by the Workgroup on this issue is required.

5   THE ENVIRONMENTAL COMPLEXITY (EC) AXIS/ASPECT

Two approaches are discussed to explore the EC metrics, a generic algorithm and domain-specific, exhaustive elaboration.

5.1 Generic, System Independent Approach

The central idea is called solution ratio, which is essentially the ratio of the number of total possible choices that a robot can make and the number of correct choices (called solutions) that meet the mission/task objectives. For example, a robot assigned a mobility task can go anywhere for many clock cycles in the middle of miles of flat benign fields. All the moves are considered correct solutions. In this case, EC = 1. If a robot gets into an environmental situation for which no correct solution can be generated, the EC is infinitely complex. If a robot is incapacitated, EC= 0/0, called undefined.

This "solution" concept could be appended with another concept, namely, the level of difficulty of a solution. When a vehicle is passing a bridge, the solution ratio may be one, but the width of the bridge could make a big difference in terms of execution. This effect should be an attribute to the solution. Another example is that, between railway and a rubble-formed tunnel, the solution ratios are both 1, but difficulty levels may be different. The following is defined for the mobility issue:

Level of Difficulty

- o *beyond the UMS's physical capability: for example, when the bridge is narrower than the width of the UMS*

- o *highly restrictive: minimal clearances, when the bridge is 5 % (or another number that practitioners identified) wider than the width of the UMS footprint or when the ditch is within a certain small percentage narrower than the UMS wheels.*

- o *restrictive: when there is clearance but still requires high level perception, planning, and execution capability*

- o *low restrictive: when there is clearance but still requires rudimentary level perception, planning, and execution capability*

- o *unrestrictive: open space and fully traversable*

Note that, when a UMS planner is searching for solutions, environmental constraints are not the only concern. Additional concerns include strategic, efficiency, and effectiveness toward mission. These should be considered outside of the EC evaluation.

Note also that, when the solutions are generated by a non-search based method, the equivalent solution ratios should be used. For example, when a state transition based method is used, the ratio of numbers of transition versus states could be used.

The EC metrics are grouped as followed:

- • Search space, solution ratio, and number of significant factors

  - o Description: The search space is defined as the robot's physical operating area with a predefined size. The solution ratio is calculated within an individual space. The metric score for the total mission environment would be cumulative of the individual solution ratios. The guidelines for defining the sizes are to be developed.

The constraints for the robotic decisions should be taken into account. For example, for a road following task, the factors should include deviation allowed from the centerline, road width and radius, speed requirements, road condition, visibility, combat concerns in military situations, etc.

o   Scale/Measure: to be defined.

- Variability of the environment

    o   Description: This set of metrics concerns the dynamics of the environment. The aforementioned constraints can change in their ranges, weights, and numbers over time and space. The changes can be due to system actions or natural progressions.

    How the factors change is also a metric, including the rates, the magnitudes, and the patterns of the changes. Road traffic changes could follow a pattern, whereas combat situations can change randomly. Representation and prediction models can be built when the changes are understood.

    Environmental factors can also change due to natural progression or system actions. For example, visibility of the road might change as the time of the day progresses or due to the dust generated by the passage of a vehicle. The road might change from two lanes to four lanes or could change to not passable after a bomb exploded.

    o   Scale/Measure: The general scales for the rate of change could be none (static environment), slow, medium, fast, but specifics are to be defined.

- Environmental Understanding--Variables or Objects Observability

    o   Description: Ability to recognize and discriminate between different factors; understanding full effect of factor on solution. The observability can change over time.
    o   Scale/Measure: number of features recognized and the fidelity of the recognized features

5.2   Categorizing Environmental Attributes

Earlier efforts for developing the EC metrics focused on detailed identification of environmental attributes, such as terrain, climate, traffic, etc. We attempted to exhaustively categorize the environmental attributes [56] and attempting to analyze their levels of difficulty or complexity. Although this approach may be too system dependent, the results facilitate EC evaluation. The UMSs' specific physical characteristics or capabilities, the equipped sensors, the perception systems, etc., may have been critical factors in determining the complexity levels.

The EC measure is decomposed in the below table. Each category is further described with a draft set of specific measurable factors. The granularity of the factors within each category must still be determined. For example, although a UMS can maneuver through smoke, the level of visibility must be determined, considering the safe speed of the vehicle. Many such inter-dependencies and issues with the detail of the measure arise. The following table represents the initial breakout of the primary categories for the EC set of measures.

Static Environment	Measure the ability of the unmanned system to operate within a known, non-moving, geo-referenced area. The categories Urban and Rural Environment also include static environment variables, but address man made static entities only. Static Environment variables include terrain type, soil characteristics, water depth, terrain elevation and elevation change characteristics.
Dynamic Environment	Assess the unmanned system's ability to detect and negotiate changes in the environment while minimizing the impact on mission goals. Dynamic Environment variable metrics include frequency of obstacles, density of obstacles, detection and use of access points, and human interaction, non-tactical changes to the environment due to system actions.
Electronic/ Electromagnetic Environment	The unmanned system's ability to communicate and function with respect to the impact of electromagnetic fields, and/or any other energy source both hostile and friendly. Specific measures to be accounted for within this category include the UMS's ability to withstand communication dropouts, jamming, magnetic fields, EMP, and multi-path.
Mobility	The impact of the environment on the UMS includes common metrics such as range, turn radius/rate, max roll/pitch, shock, vibration, acceleration and deceleration. Ideally, these measures will be collected for a full six degrees of freedom (DOF) environment.
Mapping and Navigation	The required environmental data and the associated resolutions, such as maps, elevations, etc., impact the vehicle's CAC. Also included in this category are navigational aids used by the UMS such as GPS and air traffic control interfaces.
Urban Environment	The Urban Environmental factors account for the measurable impact of traffic, road conditions, road variation, traffic rules, control points, and any other man-made mobility constraints and choices. Additional factors of the Urban Environment may be listed in other, more

	specific, categories.
Rural Environment	Rural Environment variables include vegetation, fences, walls and other barriers, and biological factors such as wildlife and domestic animals. As with the Urban Environment, other factors may be listed in other categories.
Weather	This measure accounts for variables such as sea state, wind speed, pressure, humidity, visibility (due to atmospheric conditions), lighting conditions, and any other natural phenomenon that might impact mobility.
Operational Environment	The Operational Environment differs from Mission Complexity in that it does not account for the tactical or strategic attributes of the mission, but captures the factors that force change, temporary and/or intermittent, on the mission. Factors listed within this category include enemy fire, decoys, change in the operational tempo, and enemy tactical changes to the environment based on my actions.

At this time, the Workgroup is not directly addressing specific inter-dependencies between the various measures. The granularity of the measure, however, will be proposed and used for development of the CAC model. As the model matures, many changes in both the categories and factors of the data set and the granularity of measures will occur. The population of the first draft of the EC metrics is planned. Examples are presented below to further exemplify the challenge.

Soil Characteristics	General description of the type of soil the unmanned vehicle can traverse without damage and/or loss of traction.
	Sand
	Clay
	Grass
	Rock
	Gravel
	Pebble
	Constant Mud
Terrain Elevation Change	Average change in elevation of terrain accounting for both frequency and amplitude
	Vertical Change in meters from trough to peak (0 to 10000 as an example)
	Horizontal distance in meters between peaks (0 to 10000 as an example)
Frequency of Obstacles	Determine the impact of system performance during mobility based on the occurrences of obstacles with respect to time. This measure represents the ability of the system to process sensory input into the obstacle perception, classification, and/or negotiation processes.

	Greater than 5 minutes (as an example)
	5 minutes to 120 second intervals
	...
	1 to 10 occurrences per second
	...
Density of Obstacles	Obstacle density is the measure of occurrences of anomalies within a 1000m x 1000m area. This is a measure of the number of obstacles a UMS can detect, track, and avoid (if necessary) in the determined area.
	1000
	500 to 1000
	250 to 500
	...
	less than 10

It can be seen, from this example that numerous factors appear to be left out. The type of soil, for instance, does not fully quantify the impact of that soil on the vehicle system. Clay might be easily traversable until a hard rain makes it all but impossible for a light skid-steer UMS to perform even simple maneuvers. The classification of elevation data, presented as an average for an area, would not at first glance appear to have an impact on the CAC of UMS. However, combined with minimum and maximum factors, the measure provides a basis for determining the fit of a UMS to a particular terrain. Further, we have not developed quantifiable formulas for these factors.

6 CHARACTERISTICS AND ISSUES

6.1 Correlations and Interdependency

ALFUS aims at comprehensive sets of metrics. Some of the metrics may be interrelated. Some may not be relevant to certain applications. Some metrics might be more important than other metrics in different types of applications. In many situations, using a weighted average method on the metric scores could provide an adequate indication for the CAC. However, there may well be cases when weighted minimum or maximum values might be more suitable. For example, the MC axis contains metrics for perception and tactical behavior. A low score for the perception capabilities for a UMS implies that it may not be able to support a high-level, complex, autonomous mission behavior. In this situation, the lower score between the perception and tactical behavior should be used as the requirement instead of the average.

6.2 Overlap among the Three Axes

Workshop discussions revealed that the three axes might not be totally independent. The reason for using the three-axis model is to highlight the aspects that should be included in dealing with the autonomy capabilities of UMSs.

Overlaps exist among the three axes, especially between MC and EC. The following sections described the workshop discussions on this topic.

6.1.1   MC – EC Overlap

A mission is, essentially, an operation that is performed in a particular environment. Therefore, both the operation and the environment may contribute to the complexity of the mission. Also, an environment is irrelevant without missions. Missions always involve environments.

Figure 9 could be used to illustrate the issue. If we consider the relevance of the environment to the mission, the environment could be either benign or operating space. For example, the field for a navigation mission, the rubble pile for a search mission, etc., are operating space whereas the ocean that is thousands of miles away is irrelevant. This is shown from left to right in the figure. The operating space includes object(s) of a mission, for example, walls or trees in the way for a navigation mission, or victims in a search mission. Farthest to the left is mission operation, which may be independent of the environment.

An outstanding issue in the Workgroup is to investigate setting up some guidelines for determining whether an autonomy issue should be considered as EC or MC along this spectrum.

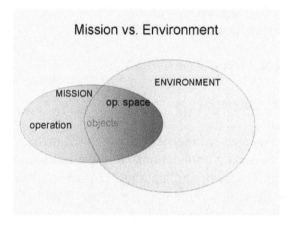

Figure 9: EC – MC Spectrum

Due to the concern, we have explored alternative views, such as attempting to combine EC and MC as a single axis, as shown in Figure 10. Nevertheless, the prevailing thoughts are that the prismatic, Figure 1, and the three-axis views, Figure 3, provide the best representation for the autonomy characterization purposes.

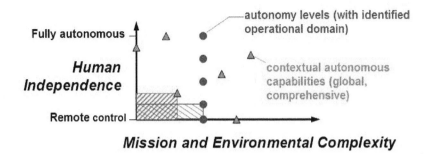

Figure 10: A Simplified ALFUS View

6.1.2 Interdependences between MC and HI and between EC and HI

It has been an ongoing issue in the ALFUS development process as whether MC levels would change depending on the levels of human interaction or would the MC be independent of the interactions. One argument was that human and UMS might handle tasks in different ways, therefore, the task decomposition might differ. This might indicate that MC is dependent on HI. However, another argument was that the requirements for performing a mission should be the same regardless of whether it is performed by UMSs or humans. This seems to indicate that MC should be independent of HI.

Similarly, between HI and EC, environmental complexity might or might not differ between when humans or when UMSs are operating. An additional issue would be whether the operator is stationary or on the move. The environments could affect the HI performance. For supporting evidence, see [86, 87, 88]

These issues remain to be further analyzed.

6.3 Context

An issue warranting further development is context. In other words, should the ALFUS levels be applied in a global reference frame or are the levels relative measures? A common question asked was, does an ant have the same LOA as a UMS when both are fully autonomous? In a global reference frame, once both are independent of HRI, they might both have the highest LOA, but might have different levels of MC or EC. In relative reference frames, the LOA might be measured within the particular context. Further elaboration of this issue includes:

- Would the LOA or the overall CAC be lowered due to the fact that a UGV cannot fly or a UMS cannot perform a mission for lack of onboard equipment?

- Would the overall CAC for a large UGV be higher than a small UGV for being able to cross wide ditches, but, meanwhile, lower for not being able to cross narrow bridges? Would the overall CAC for an amphibious UMS be higher than a UGV or USV?

The above seem to point to either relative or context based autonomy evaluations. If so, then the next issue is the categorizations of UMSs or environments within which autonomy are compared or evaluated. Examples are:

- Domain specific—UAV, UGV, USV, UUV, spacecraft

- Environment specific—Urban, off-road, swamp, icy/snowy

- UMS size based

- Mission based—RSTA, public transportation

- Program specific

A further question is, what is the proper level of details with this categorization scheme? For example, would it be always beneficial to further divide UAV into fixed-wing and rotor-based aircrafts? This warrants further investigation so that a set of guidelines can be established in the ALFUS Framework.

Context is important during the application of ALFUS. It would be prudent for a program to specify its LOA requirements once the missions and the performing environments are understood. An ant and a UMS might have the same number indicating the LOA, but the contexts are totally different. Comparisons of CAC among different programs might or might not be feasible.

The EC axis has the similar issue. A particular environment might be difficult for some UMSs but relatively easy for some other UMSs. A large UMS might cross a ditch more easily than a small one which might cross a narrow bridge more easily.

The complexity of a mission may depend on factors such as how the UMS is equipped, which may affect the task decomposition of the mission.

6.4   Measurability and Measurement Scales

The metrics need to be measurable to be useful. Determining proper scales for each metric is quite a challenge. Common scales include 0 through 10, low/med/high, minimum/low/med/high/advanced, etc. The latter two may need to be quantified for evaluations and comparisons. Proper guidelines are needed for establishing these scales.

Some of the measures are open issues and ongoing research topics. For example, a metric in HI is "operator mental workload" and a scale is assigned as low/med/high. Additional studies are needed to determine what is considered low, med, or high. Could workload be reflected by the number of the OCU screens that the operator has to handle, the number of mouse clicks or keystrokes to assist a particular task, or the percentage of time the operator could take her/his eyes off the screens?

6.5 Weights

Weights can be applied to both metrics and tasks when evaluating the UMSs' autonomous capabilities. There can be many different weight distribution scales, such as:

- Binary; used when certain metrics or tasks are applicable or non-applicable.

- Linear or logarithmic scales; users can decide how, relatively, the tasks or metrics are applicable to certain situations. Some tasks might be critical in mission performance while others might be only for information sharing purposes only. Pre-determined weight distribution can be applied accordingly. The weight distribution for the metrics can be treated similarly.

- A normal value with a certain percentage higher or lower.

- A dynamic algorithm.

Additional considerations include:

- Would the summation of weights amount to a fixed number? For example, when a task is decomposed, would the summation of the weights for all the subtasks or metrics be one, in other words:
  - $\Sigma(\text{weight}) = 1$?
  - $\Sigma(\text{weight} * \text{full metric score}) = 1$?

- In some UMSs, the planning and execution methodology already considers weights for the tasks. For example, in the NIST 4Dimension/Realtime Control System architecture, or 4D/RCS [66], the value judgment function for a control node computes the costs and benefits in task planning. These correspond to the task weights.

Further, systematic investigation is needed.

6.6 Systems and Performance, or the "Hidden/Fourth Axis"

The CAC provides an indication of the subject UMS's capability to accomplish the mission goals. This implies that the performance requirements are specified in the mission goals. Issues like tolerances, repeatability, and safety margins should be addressed in the mission goals. These issues cover both the spatial and temporal aspects.

The EC and MC levels of a UMS may be affected by the hardware that it possesses. A faster CPU, a camera with a wider field-of-view and finer resolution, or a smarter knowledge engine could make the UMS more capable. A longer arm could make the UMS more able to reach. These systems issues could be embedded in the MC and EC axes and can be reflected in the corresponding metrics.

39

Conversely, attempts could be made to explore whether these issues can be made explicit and form the "fourth axis/aspect," possibly called the "performer" axis/aspect.

From the performer perspective, the issue is centered on how complex a mission a UMS can handle:

- How many missions can a UMS handle, concurrently, sequentially, or separately?

- How much mission switching can the UMS handle?

- What are the costs for the switching, including transition time that results in loss of productivity or waste of resources?

There is also research on biologically inspired robots that calls for multifunctional material and structure, which, in turn, better emulate the performance of muscles, possess multiple desirable engineering features such as visco-elasticity and magnetism. These could enhance the CAC model [89].

These seem to indicate that a whole set of new metrics may be needed.

6.7   Nominal vs. Instantaneous Levels

The ALFUS Levels are typically used in a nominal sense for characterizing a task or a UMS. The operational and environmental situations vary as a UMS executes a mission. As such, the instantaneous CAC, including MC, EC, and HI (or LOA) value may vary along the course. Note that defining the nominal versus dynamic natures of ALFUS is still an open issue in the Workgroup.

7   GUIDELINES AND PROCESSES

Guidelines and processes are needed for the application of the ALFUS Framework. There are several methods that are being explored: directly applying the metrics, analyzing autonomy through its definition, and determining task/mission complexity by filtering up the ALFUS levels from the lower levels.

7.1 CAC Model Process

In ALFUS, the autonomous capability of UMS is evaluated with the three sets of metrics.

7.1.1   Evaluation Process

The individual metrics are applied to a mission that the UMS is assigned to perform. This results in the level of complexity of the mission, the level of complexity of the environment, and the level of autonomy. This process is described below:

- Identify applicable metrics and their relative weights.

- Decompose the missions into a series of levels of sub-tasks. This is called a task decomposition process. The decomposition process continues until the lowest level tasks are at sufficient levels of resolutions for the autonomy evaluation purposes.

- Apply the metrics to the lowest-level tasks.

- The metric evaluations for the higher-level tasks may be obtained by either weighted averages of the lower-level task evaluations or by applying the metrics to the high-level tasks directly. Further investigation is needed in this area.

Weights could be assigned to the metrics as well as to the axes, according to their criticality to individual programs. Further development effort is required for a set of comprehensive guidelines for the weight distribution. For now, the weights that can be used are zero and one. A weight of zero indicates that the metric is irrelevant.

Weights can also be assigned to the mission tasks, as some of the tasks might be considered more critical than the others. Similarly, before a set of guidelines is developed, the only weight that is used is one.

The metrics can be applied either top-down or bottom-up with respect to the task decomposition structure for the mission. In the bottom-up approach, a complete task decomposition of the mission is generated from top through bottom, the basic skill level. The metrics are applied to the skills and the scores are integrated up to achieve the mission complexity scores at the top level. This approach requires a comprehensive task analysis. Figure 11 demonstrates this process.

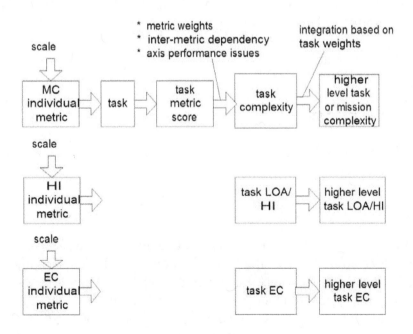

Figure 11: Illustrated ALFUS Metrics Evaluation Process

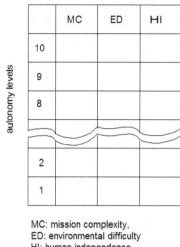

	MC	ED	HI
10			
9			
8			
2			
1			

autonomy levels

MC: mission complexity,
ED: environmental difficulty
HI: human independence

Figure 12: ALFUS Metric Scores

In the case when a system is being conceptualized and complete task decomposition is not feasible, a top-down approach is conceivable. The approach calls for the metrics to be applied to the first level of task decomposition of the mission.

A standard task decomposition method is, therefore, extremely helpful. The NIST 4D/RCS task analysis process is suitable for the process [90].

Another issue area is about the confidence level and perturbation for the autonomy capability evaluation, i.e., sensitivity of the outcome to small changes in the input data or the environment. Further investigation is required.

7.1.2   Additional Representations

Explicit representation of the three axis scores might be helpful in some situations. Figure 12 provides an example with the metric scores for the three axes shown.

The autonomy level representation can also be associated with uncertainty and/or statistical attributes.

7.2   Layers of Details of the Framework

As described in the earlier sections, multiple layers of details can be devised in ALFUS to provide proper levels of abstraction for the UMS autonomy, as illustrated in Figure 13. The higher layers facilitate requirements specification and communication purposes, whereas the lower levels facilitate implementation and testing and evaluation. Note that the single number index for CAC, located at the far left, is grayed out as the general consensus is that it is over simplified in terms of providing autonomy information.

These layers of details are not to be confused with hierarchical control levels.

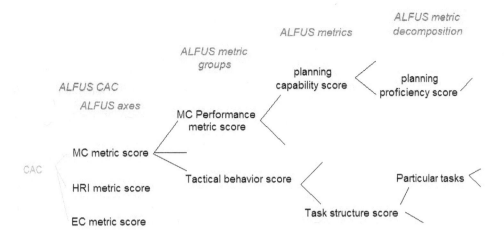

Figure 13: Layers of Details

7.3 Fixing Three Tasking Levels

The brainstorming sessions in the Framework development process have generated many possible approaches for the characterization of UMS autonomy. One of them is to limit the task decomposition to three levels, namely, group tasks, individual vehicle tasks, and subsystem tasks which are equivalent to the skills. The group tasks and the subsystem tasks can be further decomposed using a traditional hierarchical method to evaluate their levels of complexity.

Further investigation is required for this approach.

7.4 Tool

The Workgroup sees the advantage of a software tool. The central concept for the tool is automatic calculation of metric scores for the identified missions, tasks, or unmanned systems. Figure 14 illustrates the tool using a Mission Complexity example. The leftmost section of the spreadsheet contains the hierarchical task decomposition of a mission. In this example, the mission is to Conduct_Route_Reconn. Its main subtasks include Tactically_Follow and Reconn_Avenue_of_Approach. This is only a small part of the complete task structure.

Each of the lowest level subtasks (level 2, in this example) is evaluated against all the three sets of the ALFUS metrics (illustrated in the middle columns of the figure, only two metrics were shown). These scores are weighted and averaged to form a composite score for the subtasks (shown in the rightmost section of the figure, for example, the score for the Move_to_Standoff_Position subtask is (6 * 1 + 8 * 1.2) / 2 = 7.8).

Task decomposition			Subtask metric scores and weights				Hierarchical task score results and weights				
mission	Subtask level 1	Subtask level 2 ...	Metric #1	metric weight	Metric #2 ...	metric weight ...	subtask score	subtask weight	higher task agg. score	higher task weight	...
Route Recon											
	Tactically Follow								5.6	1.4	
		Move To Standoff Position	6	1	8	1.2	7.8	1			
		Turn Onto Road	4	1	3	0.9	3.4	1			
		...									
	Recon Avenue of Approach										
	...										

Figure 14: ALFUS Tool Illustration

The subtask scores are further weighted and averaged to provide the composite scores for the next higher-level tasks (for Tactically_Follow, in the example). This process continues until the mission gets its composite score.

The ALFUS framework has been going through many evolutions. Once consensus on the metrics is reached, we could easily update the tool. Therefore, currently, we have not been focusing on updating the tool.

reference levels:	reference metrics summaries			ALFUS Levels
	MC	**EC**	**HI**	**User-defined levels using metrics summaries to the left**
10	highest adaptation, decision space, team of teams collaborative missions; fully real-time planning; omniscient, highest level fidelity SA; human level performance	lowest solution/possibility ratio: lowest margin for error, understandability; highest level of dynamics, variation, risks, uncertainty, mechanical constraints*	performing on its own and approaching zero human interaction, negotiating with appropriate individuals	
9	high adaptation, decision space, team collaborative missions/tasks; high real-time planning; strategic level, high fidelity SA	low solution/possibility ratio, understandability highly dynamic, complex, adversarial high risks, uncertainty, constraints*	UMS informs humans; human provides strategic goals, interacting time between 6 % and 35 %;	
8				
7				
6	limited adaptation, decision space, vehicle tasking; limited real-time planning; tactical level, mid fidelity SA	mid solution/possibility ratio, understandability dynamic, simple mid risks, uncertainty, constraints*	human approves decisions, provides tactical goals, interacting time between 36 % and 65 %	
5				
4				
3	subsystem tasks/skills; internal, low fidelity SA	high solution/possibility ratio, understandability static, simple low risks, uncertainty, constraints*	human decides, provides waypoints, interacting time between 66 % & 95 %	
2				
1				
0	simplest, binary tasks	static, simple	remote control	

Table 1: Intermediate Metric Summaries for the Executive Model

7.5 Executive Model—Metrics Based Approach

As described earlier, the objective of the executive or summary model is to provide a set of definitions to facilitate high-level communication on UMS autonomy. The definitions of the individual metrics are integrated through multiple stages to provide definitions for the autonomy levels.

This approach for the executive model is to provide intermediate metric summaries as references. ALFUS levels are defined for the applications based on the summaries. This is shown in Table 1. Users have the discretion of determining or defining the ALFUS levels given the intermediate summaries, shown on the left of the table.

Alternatively, the Workshops could explore defining the levels reference by referring to the intermediate summaries. Appendix C describes some of the evolving concepts.

7.5.1 Autonomy Capability Tradeoff

An interesting issue is whether tradeoffs among the three axes provide comparative capabilities per the UMS goals. For example, during the design phase, would it be a consideration to select ($MC = 5$; $EC = 5$; $HI = 5$), ($MC = 2$; $EC = 5$; $HI = 8$), or ($MC = 7$; $EC = 2$; $HI = 6$), all sum up to be 15?

It remains to be investigated whether the summary number provides useful indication for the CAC. If so, then cost and benefit analysis can be conducted on trading off among the three axes. Appendix B provides a model.

7.6 Executive Model—Key Definition Based Approach

Based on the structure of the ALFUS Framework as described in Figure 2, it is feasible to use the key definitions of Autonomy and RAC to define the ALFUS levels, including level of HI (LOA), level of MC, and level of EC. This approach could complement what were described in Sections 2 through 5, the metrics-based approach.

The following sections elaborate these concepts in detail. FCS LSI has presented this approach and used it to define LOA [91] in the recent ALFUS Workshops. Appendix A provides an illustration.

7.6.1 Level of Autonomy

The LOA corresponds to the HI axis of the Framework. In Section 5, we described that the LOA is higher when the corresponding metrics yield higher scores. In this section, we further describe that higher HI scores indicate that the RACs, namely, sensing, perceiving, analyzing, communicating, planning, decision-making, and acting are performed by the UMS to higher extents. In other words, LOA is higher when the RACs are performed by the UMS to higher extents.

The correspondences between the RACs and the metrics must be established. The following is an attempt:

Sensing, Perception: A higher level of participation by the UMS may correspond to lower scores in the metrics of human intervention ratio and human workload and higher scores for the robotic independence and higher robotic initiation metrics.

Analyzing, Planning, Decision-making: A higher level of participation by the UMS may correspond to lower metric scores for human planning ratio and human workload and higher scores for robotic independence and higher robotic initiation.

Acting/Executing: A higher level of participation by the UMS may correspond to lower metric scores for human intervention ratio and human workload and higher scores for robotic independence and higher robotic initiation.

Communicating: A higher level of participation by the UMS may correspond to lower metric scores for human intervention ratio, commanding level, and human workload and higher scores for robotic independence and higher robotic initiation.

The RACs should be an integrated set and that a collection of the isolated functions might not facilitate system's autonomy.

Figure 15 illustrates this correspondence effort. See Section 4 for the discussions of the metrics.

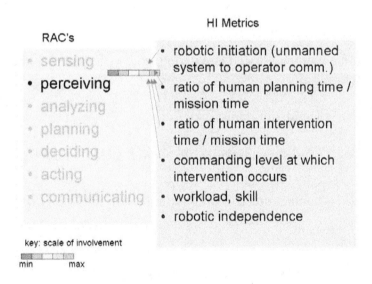

Figure 15: Root Autonomous Capabilities Based Approach

7.6.2   LOA Reference, Conceptual Definitions

Since LOA is based on the degrees of the UMS involvement or the levels of the UMS efforts in performing the RACs, the modes of the UMS operations, i.e., remote control, teleoperation, semi-autonomous, and fully autonomous can provide a basis for the LOA definitions.

Different operator roles, defined in detail in the ALFUS terminology [1], could also facilitate the AL identifications. The roles include:

- Supervisor
- Teammate
- Operator
- Mechanic or Developer
- Bystander

The first three roles concern LOA.

Different types of HRI, also defined in ALFUS to facilitate the LOA identifications, include:

- Human Operated
- Human Assisted
- Human Delegated
- Human Supervised

These definitions take into account the degrees of human involvement or amounts of efforts, in terms of time and efforts. Additional terms such as Human Guided, Human Directed, etc. are also used in the community.

From these and from the aforementioned key definitions, we summarize the following approach for LOA definition:

First, the reference LOAs are identified as:

- RC/Teleoperation—human, while off-board the UMS, directly controls all of the RACs.
- Human lead—human directly controls more than the UMS does of the RACs.
- Shared—human and the UMS directly control the RACs at equivalent levels of effort.
- UMS lead—the UMS controls more than human does.
- Fully autonomous—UMS performs all of the RACs.

Second, the guidelines for the LOA definition process are:

1. Certain ranges of flexibility exist in terms of the levels of effort of direct control. For example, by Shared, instead of precise 50 % contribution from human and the UMS, it should be anywhere between 45 % and 55 % or another range specified by individual Programs.

2. Individual Programs can interpolate the reference LOAs for additional levels. For example, the following are possible sets of LOAs:

(Set A)

- RC
- Teleoperation
- Human directed
- Human lead
- Shared
- UMS lead
- UMS directed
- Fully autonomous

(Set B)

- Remote control
- Advanced remote control
- Teleoperation
- Human guided
- Advanced human guided
- Human UMS shared
- Human delegated
- Advanced human delegated
- UMS guided
- Advanced UMS guided
- Fully autonomous

3. The differentiations among the consecutive LOAs do not have to be linear. Some suggested that a logarithmic scale of the degrees of involvement be used for level identification, which warrants further exploration. Along the same line of reasoning, the LOA axis does not have to be symmetric off the Shared level. In other words, the level at which human and UMS equally share the operation does not necessarily have to be at the middle level of a LOA scale.

4. Human centric view vs. UMS centric view: In a human centric view, humans could participate in the operation all the time. However, this does not necessarily mean that

all the UMS RACs are performed by humans. Therefore, the LOA should be defined in terms of UMS participation levels.

This approach facilitates individual programs to extend for their autonomy level definitions. FCS LSI has been participating in the ALFUS workshops and presented and proposed its analysis [91]. LSI identified the autonomy levels as, from high to low: Autonomous, Human Aided, Human Directed, Teleoperation, and Remote Control. Appendix A provides an illustration. This set of LOA is consistent with the model as described in this section, as well as consistent with the aforementioned approach of extending the specific model from the generic model, in Section 2.5.

7.6.3 Mission Complexity

In Section 3, we described that the complexity for a mission to be evaluated is higher when the corresponding metrics yield higher scores. In this section, we further describe that higher MC metric scores indicate that the RACs are more complex.

The correspondences between the RACs and the metrics are established as the following:

1. Sensing and Perception: A more complex mission, evaluated through the MC metrics, generally requires more complex sensory and perceptual data.

2. Analyzing, Planning, Decision-making: A more complex mission, evaluated through the MC metrics, generally requires more complex capabilities of these.

3. Acting/Executing: A more complex mission may require higher acting/executing capabilities, which might include emergency or failure procedures.

4. Communication: A more complex mission may require higher communication capabilities.

7.6.4 Environmental Complexity

A more difficult environment for a UMS would generally be one that is harder to sense and perceive, more difficult to analyze and plan with, harder to make decisions with and act upon, and harder to communicate within.

Therefore, the RACs correspond to the EC metrics.

8   TASK DECOMPOSITION

Task decomposition (TD) is a system development and execution paradigm that is oriented at task and command, i.e., what UMS and its components are to perform. TD contrasts with other development and execution paradigms that might be object oriented or functionally oriented. TD facilitates mission performance. It is, therefore, extremely beneficial for the tasks to be specified with required autonomy and to be evaluated to be possessing appropriate levels of CAC. A typical TD can be seen in Figure 8. A straw-man model for a hypothetical autonomous lawn mower, shown in Figure 16, was also used in the Workshop discussions.

These point to the requirement for a consistent and well-developed TD method. Earlier studies on the topic include Seels and Glasgow [92], Harrow [93], and Krathwohl et al. [94]. Task decomposition processes have been perceived as either hierarchical—prerequisite, answering what must be known or performed—or procedural—determining the physical steps which must be accomplished to assure completion. ALFUS adopts the 4D/RCS TD methodology [66, 90]. A high-level mission needs to be decomposed into low-level tasks before they are executed.

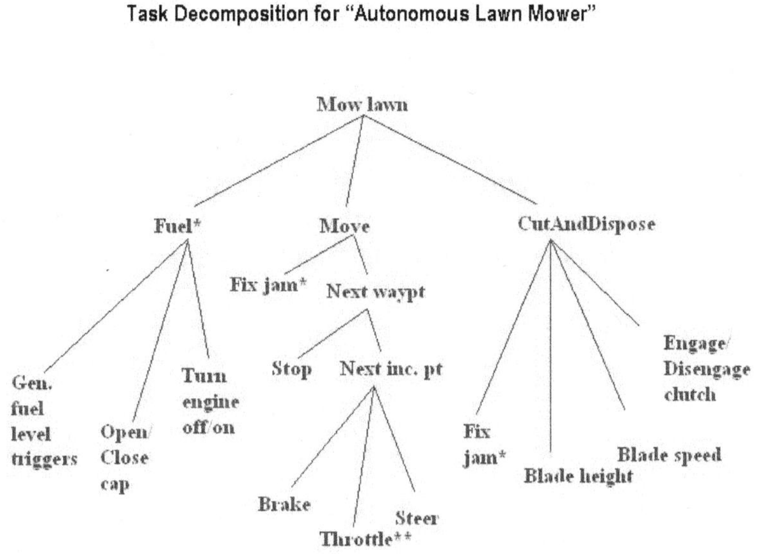

Figure 16: Conceptual TD for an Autonomous Lawn Mower

TD depends on system configuration. A task may be decomposed differently for UMSs with different capabilities. Capability differences also exist between humans and UMSs. Humans might be more suitable in handling a limited number of tasks while machines might be much less constrained by such a factor. Additional studies on this issue can be found in [95, 96, 97, 98, 99]. TD might also depend on system design method and architecture. We focus on hierarchical, real-time system control in this document.

The objective for TD, at the design phase[3], would be to identify and organize tasks for the intended operations of unmanned systems and to map the resulting task structures into a control hierarchy, as shown in Figure 17.

The control hierarchies provide the organization into which the tasks should be decomposed [100, 101], because the controller nodes plan and execute the tasks. The two hierarchies could be developed iteratively. Some other times the controller hierarchy is pre-existent and, as such, serves the constraint for the TD.

---

[3] During runtime, TD means the planning and execution of the tasks by all the control nodes of the unmanned systems.

Tasks and their decomposition are behavior oriented. The execution of the tasks generates corresponding physical behaviors. The perceptive functions supporting behavioral generation should not be considered tasks by themselves.

8.1 Attributes of a Task

8.1.1 States

Tasks should be designed as to have distinctive and clearly defined starting, final, and intermediate states. The states should facilitate design, execution, and human observability.

8.1.2 Human-Inspired Abstraction

It is desirable if tasks can be decomposed and structured at similar levels of abstraction as common human practices. For example, for the driving tasks, the stay-in-lane task and the turn-right task may be essential at a mid level of abstraction. At a lower level, the properly decomposed tasks would include steering angles and throttle positions.

8.1.3 Task Completion

The execution of all the subtasks represents the complete execution of the parent task.

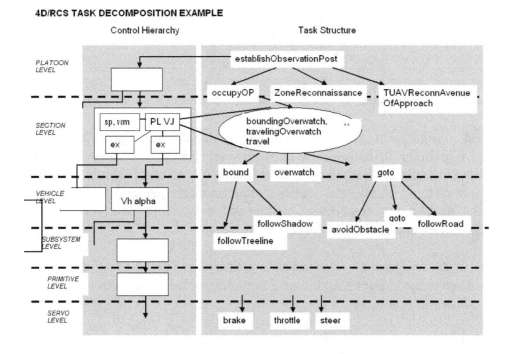

Figure 17: 4D/RCS TD Example

8.2 Guidelines for Task Decomposition

a. Tasks are decomposed with two aspects: spatial separation and temporal steps [100, 102, 103].

b. Task decomposition may be guided by the human factors of understandability, manageability, and standard tasks.

c. Tasks may be decomposed according to sets of reference levels of abstraction as defined in 4D/RCS. The levels are, top-down, mission/system/application, group, equipment/vehicle, elementary move (or major functions or subsystem), primitive move, and actuator (or servo).

   4D/RCS also features a perception hierarchy that facilitates sensory data integration. The levels are, bottom-up, data points, list, surface, object, and object group. These can be referenced during developing perception functions to facilitate the TD.

   Note that these are reference levels or types of levels. A system may need multiple group (or any other) levels to sufficiently decompose a task at those levels.

d. In performing TD, one must first identify existent "constraints," including commands or interfaces for actuators and controllers.

e. Task structure and controller hierarchy are to be developed in parallel and iteratively.

8.3 Spatial Perspective

a. Spatial TD leads to hierarchical task structures. Each layer in the task structures represents a different level of abstraction of the tasks. When a task is decomposed, the subtasks are described in a finer level of details with a narrower spatial scope.

b. TD is constrained by the performing agents, as depicted in Figure 17, but the process is not object-oriented, as the key is task and not object. TD is not functionally oriented, either, as which might lead to issues like resource competition. In a UMS, performers are the hardware components and their layouts to form subsystems and systems. It is recognized that performers, agents, and hardware components may be closely corresponding to one another. TD might be largely or totally constrained by the performer/hardware configuration. Spatial TD also leads to distribution of tasks among control nodes at any control level. The following describes this process in details:

   (1) At higher levels of abstraction, typically in a distributed environment, the task decomposition should follow chain of command, operational structure, or agent organization.

   (2) Within a single control entity—the lower levels of abstraction, tasks should be decomposed per major functions (the functions are typically realized with subsystems).

   (3) The decomposed tasks could be further decomposed from the perspective of subfunctions when necessary.

(4) Tasks could be further decomposed and/or refined from additional aspects, including dynamics and transformation from global to local coordinate frames.

(5) Tasks are eventually decomposed for the lowest level performers, the actuators.

8.4 Temporal Perspective

Temporal TD involves logical breakdown of a large task into manageable sizes. Temporal TD typically involves single levels (as opposed to subtasking the lower levels).

(a) Control stability and computing load

Control stability can be facilitated when the ratio of the lengths of the control cycles between a hierarchical control level and its next lower levels is 10:1, nominally. It is, therefore, desirable for the tasks to be decomposed such that their execution can be bounded by the lengths of the control cycles.

As such, the observation and orientation processing requirements could affect the decomposition of the tasks.

(b) Logical sequencing and coordination with other tasks are key consideration in the temporal task decomposition[4].

8.5 Human Perspective

The human is an imperative part of the UMS lifecycle, from design, operation, maintenance, and through upgrade. Therefore, the following human factors should be considered in the TD:

(a) Understandability: The task analysis process often involves domain experts and the resulting task structure often reflects how experts break down and perform a high level task. Even during the fully autonomous operational mode in which the task structure may optimize UMS performance, human understandability is still important. The operator needs to be able to effectively and efficiently monitor the UMS. Otherwise, intervention, when necessary, might be hindered [104].

(b) Manageability: In any of the UMS operational modes when humans are involved, they must be able to effectively and efficiently handle the tasks [105, 106, 107, 108, 109]. Workload, as described in an earlier section, is a contributing factor.

(c) Standard tasks: The approach of standardizing tasks is often used in the application domains. They may be used in the task decomposition process, the challenge being to organize standard tasks for appropriate levels according to the guidelines.

---

[4] The actual sequencing activities are parts of the planning activities and may be represented in state diagrams or tables. Refer to [100] and is out of the scope of this document.

(d) The tasks should be sufficiently populated with knowledge supporting the execution of the tasks.

9 APPLICABILITY AND APPLICATION DOMAINS

The ALFUS Framework is an enabling facility that can be tailored or extended for individual UMS application needs. We discuss how ALFUS might be applied to particular domains.

In specifying a UMS system, the ALFUS levels, namely, the levels of autonomy, mission complexity, and environmental complexity could be used to indicate the threshold (minimal) or objective requirements.

The ALFUS levels may be applied to individual tasks, individual control nodes, individual control subsystems, or an entire control system, as illustrated in Figure 18.

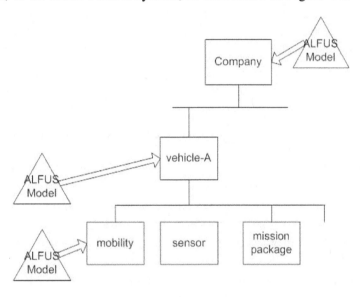

Figure 18: Applicability of ALFUS

An ongoing issue is how the ALFUS levels for tasks or missions are related to the ALFUS levels for the performing UMS:

> Would the ALFUS levels for a UMS be calculated as a weighted average of the levels of all the missions that the UMS performs?

> Would the above approach require exhaustive decomposition of all the missions operating in all required environmental conditions? If so, this would require an enormous amount of effort.

> How would the ALFUS levels for low-level tasks or control nodes be reflected at higher levels?

The following subsections describe how ALFUS might be applied to various domains.

9.1 Defense Domain

UMSs are well suited for military types of operations. UMSs can replace or support warfighters in extreme operational and environmental conditions. War fighting, surveillance, medical assistance in the field, and logistic support are just a few of the fruitful areas for UMS deployment, thus, also rich issues warranting the application of ALFUS. The following are examples of how ALFUS might be applied.

9.1.1 Requirement Specification

The Joint User community has struggled for years to find a common method of articulating its requirements. There are two major parts of the user's needs:

- A common vernacular that could be used to articulate capabilities (common set of definitions). This facilitates comparisons between systems/capabilities, and allows disparate organizations to intelligently discuss issues surrounding the use of Unmanned Systems capabilities within their operational constructs.

- A means to articulate the amount of autonomy required/expected from a UMS.

In terms of defining autonomy, the User community sees two levels of need. At an executive level, there is a need to provide a means to easily articulate requirements. This would provide a means of common communication between the User and Material Developer in expressing requirements, but would also provide an easy to understand method of explaining autonomy requirements to decision makers. At a more technical level, the User community sees a need for a tool by which interactions between the User, Material Developer, Industry, and the Test Community can be made easier. This tool could then be used to articulate system specific specification level detail and provide a framework for the testing/verification of autonomy.

The variety of autonomous systems currently envisioned for use by government and non-government entities makes a common set of terminology and definitions paramount. It also provides a challenge to the determination of the proper metrics to apply so that these definitions and metrics can be universally utilized in all the UMS domains.

9.1.2 Tactical Behavior Characterization

Tactical Behavior is defined as:

> *"The limited, near-term planning, maneuvers, and reactive procedures and actions used to adapt the execution of higher level, long term mission goals to both the environment and the operational situation, providing own unit (single or multiple elements) security and concealing mission intent from opposing forces"* [1]

Upon receiving a mission, the UMS performs task decomposition and generates a task structure for mission execution. The resulting system behaviors may include particular subsets that provide security and stealth as defined.

The specification of a UMS should include certain types of required missions and the associated tactical behaviors, which, in turn, should be specified with CAC. This would facilitate proper UMS design so that the system would be able to carry out the required missions. Tactical behavior should also be evaluated with CAC.

9.2 Manufacturing

Robots and unmanned systems can play key roles in manufacturing automation. The challenge is that a manufacturing facility could be very complex and dynamic. It could involve operators in a semi-automated facility. It receives work orders for different products with different quantities. It may need to generate various kinds of reports that contain different kinds of information for such purposes as production control, quality control, or maintenance analysis. The facility may also need to adjust its schedules to accommodate such constraints or such unexpected changes as storage or shipping. Therefore, a framework for performance measure and capability characterization should be beneficial. To begin investigating this issue, we define the following:

Logical UMS (LUMS)

An inherently non-physical and independent entity that interacts with UMSs and is considered an integrated part of the operation, such as a high-level computer control and management software system in a flexible manufacturing system (FMS), software node in a simulated UMS environment, or a conceptual entity in an analytical UMS environment

The following lists a collection of observations about potential ALFUS application:

1. An FMS, in its entirety, could be considered a UMS. Individual high level production management system software entities could be considered LUMSs when called for.

2. Production orders are equivalent to high-level missions and tasks. Machine_A_Part and Inspect_A_Part may be corresponding tasks at a middle level. Drill_A_Hole and Inspect_A_Hole may be at a low level. They could all be evaluated for the ALFUS levels.

3. Autonomous capabilities could help in characterizing many issues that a manufacturing process may encounter. Variation in the raw material in terms of composition, sizes, or weights could require adjustments of the equipment, including its settings, workload, and process flow. Equipment breakdown could also require similar adjustments. It is desirable to have the manufacturing process specified using CAC, as this would help determining whether those adjustments could be effectively handled in a human-machine coordinated way.

4. It is desirable that a manufacturing process's performance could be measured. ALFUS serves this purpose.

5. The EC could be used to characterize dynamic conditions, such as when an operator inadvertently interfered in the work volume, when a part fell off a UMS along the route, or when a machine broke down. The difficulty level could be evaluated and mission capabilities could be assessed as whether and how the situations could be handled.

57

6. The low level machining instructions correspond to the low-level UMS skills as the military UMS domain employs. The skills have different levels of difficulty, so do the machining instructions. For example, for the instruction of drilling a hole, the tolerances make differences in terms of difficulty.

7. Highly autonomous manufacturing UMS might correspond to higher initial equipment costs but lower overall lifecycle costs as well as higher capabilities for complex products.

8. Lower complexity products might mean that they are suitable for mass production using low CAC manufacturing UMSs.

9.3 Urban Search and Rescue (US&R)

One of the major concerns in US&R would be the environment. Would it be accessible? Would it be safe for responders to approach? How is an environment or an environmental condition described and conveyed to the decision maker so that the issues of concern can be resolved. Some specific examples are:

> whether an appropriately composed and equipped Emergency Response Team can be dispatched, at a certain Point of Arrival;

> whether victims are accessible, hazard material exists in the environment, the terrain is muddy or covered with snow, the water is acidic, the structure is stable, etc.

The EC levels might be used to characterize the particular environments. The environments could, in turn, be used to certify UMS for particular US&R operations. Figure 19 illustrates a US&R environment.

NIST has also embarked on an effort to establish the performance metrics for US&R robots by developing test arenas with adjustable levels of difficulty [110, 111].

Figure 19: US&R through Rubble Piles

9.4 Additional Domains and Applications

- Border Security

Variety in terrain and lengths in distance are among the challenges of securing the National borders. ALFUS could be applied to characterize the levels of complexity of the border. The results could facilitate deploying UMSs with appropriate CAC. At busy crossing ports, UMSs could help the safety related tasks such as baggage checking and identity verification. ALFUS could, in turn, help characterizing the complexity of the tasks, thus facilitating the HRI requirements specification.

- Bomb Disposal

The ultimate concern for bomb disposal would be human safety. Therefore, these types of tasks are suitable for UMS. ALFUS could, again, help analyzing the complexity of these bomb disposal operations. The analysis results could help optimize human involvement, including safe operating conditions and safe environments.

10   ALFUS FUTURE TASKS

10.1   Further Development of Framework

The immediate task for ALFUS would be to further develop the metrics. As experienced throughout the Workshops, participants still have many new ideas on what the metrics should be for each axis and how their scales should be defined. Focused efforts and systematic consensus approaches must be devised to efficiently capture the results.

Easy to use scales for the metrics must be of a high priority.

The second issue would be the Executive Model. The required effort would be to summarize the metrics and their scales to form concise definitions for the levels at the three axes.

Section 6 laid out many issues that need to be resolved, including clarifying the inter-axis overlaps, metric weight guidelines, the "fourth axis," i.e., the systems issue, and the global vs. local perspective issue.

10.2   Expansion and Generalization for Additional, Potential Benefits

The focus of the ALFUS ad hoc Workgroup has been UMS autonomy. However, it is conceivable to expand and generalize the framework for additional purposes, beyond autonomy. It is also conceivable to apply ALFUS to augment the analysis or specification of additional key concerns of UMS. The following subsections explore these opportunities.

10.2.1 General Performance Metrics Framework

The ALFUS metrics, although developed for the autonomy purposes, can be regarded as a part of the general system performance metrics.

The general performance of a UMS operator can be measured by how the operator might assist the UMS generating the plans. The operator might be measured by how heavy a workload she/he can manage. These are ALFUS HI issues—as outlined in Section 4.

A vehicle's general performance can be evaluated by how it traverses certain types of terrain and how it overcomes certain types of obstacles. These are EC issues in ALFUS.

The general performance can also be measured by how the vehicles collaborate in a team, how a UMS perceives the situations, and how the UMS revises its plans and reacts on the situations. These are among the ALFUS MC issues.

These are illustrations calling for a systematic approach to investigate generalizing the ALFUS framework for a performance metrics framework.

10.2.2 Augmenting UMS Safety Analysis with Levels of Control

The ALFUS Terminology [1] defines a term called Levels of Control that lists a series of levels, each with expanded authority for autonomous operations. This definition can be extended for the following multiple-layer safety model for a manufacturing process plant. The model contains a series of safety process design, listed from the narrower to the broader scopes [112]. The model stipulates that higher-level safety designs activate when the lower-level designs fail:

1. Design the equipment[5] and process plant to be inherently safe.
2. Design process control with safety functions.
3. Include procedures for alarms and operator intervention.
4. Include safety shut down and interlock processed for affected entities.
5. Include response mechanisms for fire and gas.
6. Include containment system for the hazards.
7. Include plant emergency response evacuation system.
8. Include community emergency response evacuation system.

The safety design at each level should be independent, yet the designs among the different levels are integrated to produce coordinated safety operations. The system configuration expands and system complexity increases from the lower to the higher levels. The following observations can be made along this process:

1. The safety operations become more complex. The complexity of safety tasks also increases as the levels increase.
2. The operating environments become broader, involve more entities, and may become more dynamic. In other words, EC increases.

---

[5] for turning, milling, drilling, forging, die-casting, rolling, etc.

60

3. Higher levels of CAC may provide for higher capabilities for safety. Yet, HRI must be carefully considered to maximize the safety.

4. A systematic approach is required for the recognition of appropriate responses subsequent to analyses, in order to develop principles for suitable response strategy [104, 113].

10.2.3 Cost Saving Through UMS Simulation

It is well understood that simulation can save UMS development costs. We explored how ALFUS could facilitate UMS simulation.

ALFUS can be used to specify a UMS. Once completed, the specification can be used as a part of the design criteria to develop the corresponding LUMS in a simulation environment. The LUMS can be used to test the CAC of the to-be-developed UMS to find out whether the specification is adequate.

A general UMS simulation environment can be designed such that the user can adjust operating environment to simulate various EC levels. For example, the pavement types of the roads, the slopes of the hills, the density of the traffic, etc., can be adjusted to evaluate how the LUMS could handle the conditions.

The mission could be scripted to the desired levels of complexity, as well. Attributes such as the number of LUMSs in a team, the command structure, the sensory capabilities, the accuracy of the goals, etc., could be designed as adjustable according to the MC levels as defined per the ALFUS metrics. This could facilitate the experimentation of the LUMS according to the desired levels of MC.

Similarly, an ALFUS enabled HRI could be developed for a simulator such that the levels of human interaction time could be tested, the types of interactions that the LUMS could initiate could be analyzed, etc. The HRI displays could be used to simulate different levels of stress that the displays might have caused the operator.

10.3 Standard Classification of Missions and Tasks

Classification of jobs or tasks is often used for humans [114, 115, 116]. It may worth exploring similar approaches for UMS. For a particular program or application, tasks or typical scenarios can be collected and evaluated for CAC, i.e., their complexities and HI. The information could be maintained in a database. When a situation arises that calls for the deployment of a UMS, the situation could be analyzed and a UMS with the matching CAC could be identified and deployed to effectively handle the situation.

11 SUMMARY

The ALFUS Framework is developed to facilitate articulating, communicating, evaluating, and documenting UMS requirements and capabilities. ALFUS identifies that HI, or human independence or levels of autonomy, MC, or mission complexity, and EC, or environmental complexity as the three aspects or axes with which the CAC, or Contextual Autonomous Capabilities for UMSs are specified. Each of the aspects is further elaborated with a set of metrics.

ALFUS also conceives a definition based Executive Model that facilitates communication of UMS autonomy in the user or application communities.

The Framework is intended to be:

> generic and covering many UMS domains, including air, ground, space, surface, and underwater; also covering many application areas, including military, homeland security, industrial, and living assistance,
>
> applicable to the full range of autonomy, from remote control through full autonomy,
>
> extensible, applicable to subsystems, single UMSs, through teams and joint missions,
>
> capable of augmenting UMS benefits of human safety and performance enhancement.

This document describes the initial version of the ALFUS Framework. Further development is required to achieve these features. Feedback from the community would be very helpful to advance the Framework.

COMPANY / PRODUCT DISCLAIMER

Certain commercial products or company names are identified in this document to describe our study adequately. In no case does such identification imply recommendation or endorsement by the National Institute of Standards and Technology, nor does it imply that the products or names identified are necessarily the best available for the purpose.

APPENDIX A: LEVEL OF AUTONOMY USE CASE

The following figure illustrates FCS LSI's LOA development work, which is consistent with the process described in Section 7.6.1 As shown on the right-hand side of the figure, the RACs migrate from to be performed by humans to by UMSs as the LOA moves higher.

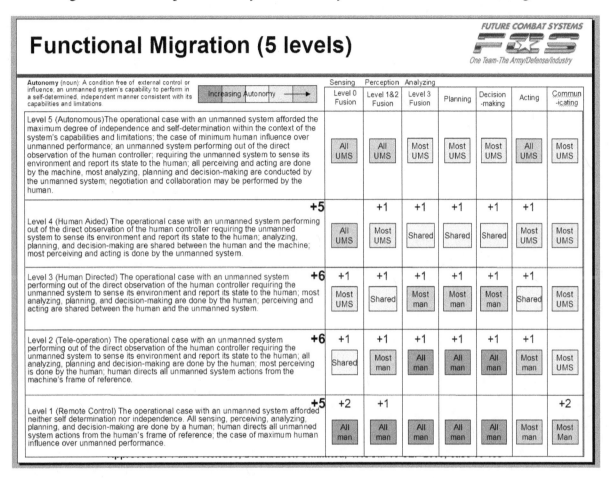

Figure A-1: FCS LSI LOA Illustration

APPENDIX B: HISTORICAL NOTES

- In its First Workshop, LOA was defined with the three-axis model of ALFUS for the purposes of covering a comprehensive scope for UMS autonomy. We later adopt the convention that LOA involves the HI axis and the three-axis model is now called CAC.

- The HI axis was originally called Human Robot Interaction (HRI). It was later changed to HI so that the direction of increasing is consistent with the other two axes.

- One of the axes, for environment, was originally called Environmental Difficulty (ED), which was determined to be too subjective and was changed to Environmental Complexity (EC).

- There were concerns that MC and EC may be too tightly coupled and might be combined into one axis. We determined to continue using the three axes.

- The Detailed Model is renamed as the Metric Model.

Workshop History

Inaugural Workshop (July 18, 2003, NIST) –Established Workgroup Objectives.

Second (September 11, 2003, BWI)—Identified Terms and started definitions.

Third (November 22, 2003, SRS Tech., Arlington, VA)—Identified metrics. Terminology published.

Fourth (February 25-26, 2004, Titan Sys., Huntsville, AL)—Identified Executive Model representation.

Fifth (May 3-4, 2004, Atlanta Airport, GA)—Metrics and measures presented. Began Interaction with FCS

Sixth (July 28-29, 2004, FCS LSI, Huntsville, GA)—Tool conceptualized.

Seventh (October 19-20, 2004, AFRL, Dayton, Ohio)—Tool updated. Began Summary Model.

Eighth (February 8 - 9, 2005, NIST, Gaithersburg, Maryland)—Continued developing Models. NIST 4D/RCS Task Analysis Method Presented. DOT ITS Briefed.

Ninth (May 4-5, 2005, TARDEC, Warren, Michigan)—Focused on metric scale development. TARDEC programs presented. ASBS and UACO Programs Briefed.

Tenth (July 20-21, 2005, U.S. Army Futures Center Forward, Arlington, Virginia)— Further development on metric scales. Additional representation presented.

Eleventh (October 25-26, 2005, U.S. Army Aviation Applied Technology Directorate, Ft. Eustis, VA).

Twelfth (February 21-22, 2006, AFRL, Dayton, OH).

Thirteenth (May 23-24, 2006, UAMBL, Ft. Knox, Kentucky).

Fourteenth (September 19-20, 2006, U.S. Navy NSWCCD Combatant Craft Dept, Ft. Monroe, Virginia).

Fifteenth (January 18-19, 2007, NIST, Gaithersburg, MD).

Sixteenth (April 24-25, 2007, Idaho National Labs, Idaho Falls City, Idaho)

Seventeenth (August 28 – 29, 2007, NIST, Gaithersburg, MD)—Co-located with 2007 Performance Metrics for Intelligent Systems (PerMIS) Workshop.

APPENDIX C: AUTONOMY CAPABILITY TRADEOFF HYPOTHESES

Table C-1 illustrates possibilities of tradeoffs among the three ALFUS axes to achieve the same total scores for CAC, given the hypothesis that every notch in the three scales carries the same weight of CAC.

Numerical scores zero through three are assigned for levels zero through nine. Users can, based on their evaluations, add up the scores for the three axes for the level number. For example, when MC = 3, EC = 0, HI = 2, the CAC total score would be five. These are further illustrated in Figure C-1.

The reason that the lowest and the highest levels are left not combined with the intermediate levels is that these two levels provide clear upper and lower bounds for the autonomy spectrum and their definitions are rather commonly understood in the community. Plus, the highest level is left independent since it is regarded as an ultimate goal for autonomy.

Ref. level	reference metrics summaries			method 2 for Level	
	MC	EC	HI	based on axis scores	
	weight	weight	weight	axis intermediate scale	sum of 3 scores
10	highest adaptation, decision space, team of teams collaborative missions; fully real-time planning; omniscient, highest level fidelity SA; human level performance	lowest solution/possibility ratio: lowest margin for error, understandability; highest level of dynamics, variation, risks, uncertainty, mechanical constraints*	performing on its own and approaching zero human interaction, negotiating with appropriate individuals	10	10
9	high adaptation, decision space, team collaborative missions/tasks; high real-time planning; strategic level, high fidelity SA	low solution/possibility ratio, understandability highly dynamic, complex, adversarial high risks, uncertainty, constraints*	UMS informs humans; human provides strategic goals, interacting time between 6 % and 35 %	3	9 (3+3+3)
8					8 (3+2+3)
7					7 (3+2+2)
6	limited adaptation, decision space, vehicle tasking; limited real-time planning; tactical level, mid fidelity	mid solution/possibility ratio, understandability dynamic, simple mid risks,	human approves decisions, provides tactical goals, interacting time between 36 % and 65 %	2	6 (3+2+1, 2+2+2, 3+3+0)
5					5 (3+1+1, 2+2+1)

67

4	SA uncertainty, constraints*				4 (2+1+1, 3+1+0)
3	subsystem tasks/skills; internal, low fidelity SA	high solution/possibility ratio, understandability static, simple low risks, uncertainty, constraints*	human decides, provides waypoints, interacting time between 66 % & 95 %	1	3 (3+0+0, 2+1+0, 1+1+1)
2					2 (2+0+0, 1+1+0)
1					1 (1+0+0)
0	simplest, binary tasks	static, simple	remote control	0	0 (0+0+0)

Table C-1: Executive Model Evolving Concept

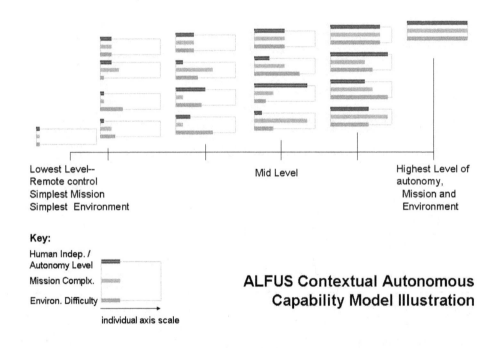

Lowest Level--
Remote control
Simplest Mission
Simplest Environment

Mid Level

Highest Level of
autonomy,
Mission and
Environment

Key:

Human Indep. /
Autonomy Level

Mission Complx.

Environ. Difficulty

individual axis scale

**ALFUS Contextual Autonomous
Capability Model Illustration**

Figure C-1: Further ALFUS CAC Illustration

REFERENCES

1   *Autonomy Levels for Unmanned Systems Framework, Volume I: Terminology, Version 1.1*, Huang, H. Ed., NIST Special Publication 1011, National Institute of Standards and Technology, Gaithersburg, MD, September 2004.

2   http://astm.org.

3   U.S. DoD OUSD Acquisition, Technology and Logistics (AT&L) Systems and Software Engineering/Developmental Test and Evaluation (OUSD (AT&L) SSE/DTE), *Unmanned Systems Safety Guide for DoD Acquisition*, January 2007.

4   http://www.jauswg.org/.

5   http://www.sae.org/.

6   http://www.isd.mel.nist.gov/US&R_Robot_Standards/.

7   2006 U.S. Army Unmanned and Autonomous Systems Testing Broad Agency Announcement.

8   http://www.army.mil/fcs/.

9   Bloss R., "By Air, Land and Sea, the Unmanned Vehicles Are Coming," Industrial Robot-An International Journal 34 (1): 12-16, Emerald Group Publishing Limited, W Yorkshire, England. 2007.

10 Albus, J., et al., "Learning in a Hierarchical Control System: 4D/RCS in the DARPA LAGR Program," Journal Of Field Robotics 23 (11-12): 975-1003 Nov-Dec, 2006, John Wiley & Sons, Hoboken, NJ, 2006.

11 http://www.nist.gov/director/states/la/fy04_la_1.htm.

12 Stormont, D.P., "Autonomous rescue robot swarms for first responders," 2005 IEEE International Conference on Computational Intelligence for Homeland Security and Personal Safety, Orlando, FL, USA, March 2005.

13 Jacoff, A., et al., "Test Arenas and Performance Metrics for Urban Search and Rescue Robots," Proceedings of the IEEE/RSJ International Conference on Intelligent Robots and Systems, Las Vegas, NV, October 2003.

14 Murphy, R., et al., "AAAI/RoboCup-2001 urban search and rescue events - Reality and competition," AI Magazine 23 (1): 37-42, 2002, Amer Assoc Artificial Intell, Menlo Pk, CA, Spring 2002.

15 Zhu, Z.G. and Hanson A.R., "Mosaic-Based 3d Scene Representation And Rendering," Signal Processing-Image Communication 21 (9): 739-754 Oct 2006, Elsevier Science BV, Amsterdam, Netherlands, 2006.

16 Carroll, D. M., et al., "Development and testing for physical security robots," Proceedings of SPIE, Volume 5804, Unmanned Ground Vehicle Technology, Orlando, Florida, March 2005.

17 http://www.cbp.gov/xp/CustomsToday/2004/Aug/other/aerial_vehicles.xml.

18 Naeem, W., et al., "Chemical plume tracing and odour source localisation by autonomous vehicles," Journal of Navigation 60 (2): 173-190, 2007, Cambridge Univ. Press, NY, NY, USA MAY 2007.

19 https://www.npdc.navy.mil/ceneoddive/eods/.

20 http://www.army.mod.uk/royalengineers/org/33regt/index.htm.

21 Da Silva, B.C., et al., "ITSUMO: An intelligent transportation system for urban mobility," Innovative Internet Community Systems Lecture Notes in Computer Science 3473: 224-235 2006.

22 Maimone, M., et al., "Two Years of Visual Odometry on the Mars Exploration Rovers," Journal of Field Robotics 24 (3): 169-186 Mar 2007, Journal of Field Robotics 23 (3-4): 245-267 Mar-Apr 2006, John Wiley & Sons Hoboken, NJ, 2007.

23 Montgomery, J., et al., "The Jet Propulsion Laboratory Autonomous Helicopter Testbed: A Platform For Planetary Exploration Technology Research And Development," Journal of Field Robotics 23 (3-4): 245-267 Mar-Apr 2006, John Wiley & Sons Hoboken, NJ, 2006.

24 Albus, J.S., "Intelligent Systems for Construction and Long Range Exploration on Planetary Surfaces," Proceedings of the American Institute of Aeronautics and Astronautics, Arlington, VA, September 26-29, 2005.

25 Boissy, P., et al., "A qualitative study of in-home robotic telepresence for home care of community-living elderly subjects," Journal of Telemedicine and Telecare 13 (2): 79-84, Royal Soc. Medicine Press Ltd., 2007.

26 Jardon, A., et al., "A Portable Light-Weight Climbing Robot for Personal Assistance Applications," Industrial Robot-an International Journal 33 (4): 303-307, Emerald Group Publishing Ltd., England, 2006.

27 Valencia-Garcia R., et al., "An Intelligent Framework for Simulating Robot-Assisted Surgical Operations," Expert Systems with Applications 28 (3): 425-433, Pergamon-Elsevier Science Ltd, England, APR 2005.

28 Okamura A.M., "Methods for haptic feedback in teleoperated robot-assisted surgery," Industrial Robot-an International Journal 31 (6): 499-508, Emerald Group Publishing Ltd., 2004.

29 Messina, E., Jacoff, A., "Performance Standards for Urban Search and Rescue Robots," Proceedings of the SPIE Defense and Security Symposium, Orlando, FL, April 2006.

30 Messina, E., et al., *"Performance Measures for Intelligent Systems: Measures of Technology Readiness PerMIS 03 White Paper,"* Proceedings of the 2003 Performance Metrics for Intelligent Systems (PerMIS) Workshop, NIST Special Publication 1014, Gaithersburg, MD, August, 2003.

31 Balakirsky, S.B., Messina, E., "A Simulation Framework for Evaluating Mobile Robots," Proceedings of the Performance Metrics for Intelligent Systems (PerMIS) Workshop, NIST Special Publication 990, Gaithersburg, MD, August 13-15, 2002.

32 http://www.jointrobotics.com/.

33 U.S. DOD, *Unmanned Aircraft Systems Roadmap 2005-2030*, http://www.acq.osd.mil/usd/Roadmap%20Final2.pdf .

34 U.S. DOD, Joint Robotics Master Plan, http://www.jointrobotics.com/activities_new/FY2003%20Joint%20Robotics%20Master%20Plan.pdf

35 Bruce T. Clough , "Metrics, Schmetrics! How The Heck Do You Determine A UAV's Autonomy Anyway?" Proceedings of the Performance Metrics for Intelligent Systems Workshop, NIST Special Publication 990, Gaithersburg, Maryland, 2002.

36 Army Science Board, Ad Hoc Study on Human Robot Interface Issues, Arlington, Virginia, 2002.

37 Da Silva, BC, et al., "ITSUMO: An intelligent transportation system for urban mobility ," Innovative Internet Community Systems Lecture Notes in Computer Science 3473: 224-235 2006.

38 Proud, R.W., et al., "Methods for Determining the Level of Autonomy to Design into a Human Spaceflight Vehicle: A Function Specific Approach," Proceedings of the Performance Metrics for Intelligent Systems (PerMIS) Workshop, Gaithersburg, MD, September, 2003.

39 Parasuraman, R., et al., "A Model For Types and Levels of Human Interaction with Automation," IEEE Transactions on Systems, Man and Cybernetics, Part A, Volume: 30 , Issue: 3, May 2000.

40 *Agent Autonomy*, Hexmoor, H., et. al, Ed., Kluwer Academic Publishers, The Neitherlands, 2003

41 Sheridan, T. B. *Telerobotics, Automation, and Human Supervisory Control*, the MIT Press. 1992.

42 Zeigler, B.P., "High autonomy systems: concepts and models," AI, Simulation, and Planning in High Autonomy Systems, 1990, Proceedings, 26-27 Mar 1990.

43 Bruemmer, D., et al., "Components of swarm intelligence," Conference on Robotics and Remote Systems-Proceedings, v 10, 10th International Conference on Robotics and Remote Systems for Hazardous Environments, 2004.

44 Bruemmer, D. J., et al., "Supporting Complex Robot Behaviors with Simple Interaction Tools." *Human Robot Interaction,* ed. Nilanjan Sarkar, Advanced Robotics Systems International, Vienna, Austria, 2007.

45 Goodrich, M., et al., "Report on the First International Conference on Human-Robot Interaction (HRI)" *AI Magazine,* v 27, n 3, Fall, 2006, p 103-104, Amer Assoc Artificial Intell, Menlo Pk, CA, 2006.

46 Bruemmer, D. J., et al., "Shared Understanding for Collaborative Control." IEEE Transactions on Systems, Man, and Cybernetics, Part A. Systems and Humans, vol. 35, no.4, pp. 505-512, Jul. 2005.

47 Marble, J., et al., "Challenges in the Design and Conduct of Usability Testing of Human-Robot Control Architectures," Conference on Robotics and Remote Systems- Proceedings, v 10, 10th International Conference on Robotics and Remote Systems for Hazardous Environments, 2004

48 Park, S. and Sheridan, T.B., "Enhanced Human-Machine Interface in Braking," IEEE Transactions on Systems, Man and Cybernetics, Part A, Volume: 34 , Issue: 5, September, 2004.

49 Yanco, H.A. and Drury, J.L., "A Taxonomy for Human-Robot Interaction," AAAI Fall Sympopsium on human-Robot Interaction, AAAI Technical Report FS-02-03, pp. 111-119, November 2002.

50 Fong, T. et al., "Common Metrics for Human-Robot Interaction," Proceedings of the IEEE 2004 International Conference on Intelligent Robots and Systems, Sendai, Japan, 2004.

51 Huang, H., et al., "Characterizing Unmanned System Autonomy: Contextual Autonomous Capability and Level of Autonomy Analyses," Proceedings of the SPIE Defense and Security Symposium 2007, Orlando, Florida, March 2007.

52 Huang, H., "The Autonomy Levels for Unmanned Systems (ALFUS) Framework--Interim Results," Proceedings of the Performance Metrics for Intelligent Systems (PerMIS) Workshop, NIST Special Publication 1062, Gaithersburg, MD, August 2006.

53 Huang, H., et al., "A Framework For Autonomy Levels For Unmanned Systems (ALFUS)," Proceedings of the AUVSI's Unmanned Systems North America Symposium, Baltimore, MD, June 2005.

54 Huang, H., et al., "Autonomy Levels for Unmanned Systems (ALFUS) Framework: An Update," Proceedings of the SPIE Defense and Security Symposium 2005, Conference 5804, Orlando, Florida, March 2005.

55 Huang, H., et al., "Autonomy Measures for Robots," Proceedings of the 2004 ASME International Mechanical Engineering Congress & Exposition, Anaheim, California, November 2004.

56 Huang, H., et al., "Specifying Autonomy Levels for Unmanned Systems: Interim Report," SPIE Defense and Security Symposium 2004, Conference 5422, Orlando, Florida, April 2004.

57 Huang, H., et al., "Toward a Generic Model for Autonomy Levels for Unmanned Systems," Proceedings of the Performance Metrics for Intelligent Systems (PerMIS) Workshop, NIST Special Publication 1014, September 16-18, 2003, Gaithersburg, MD.

58 Bruemmer, D., et al., "Shared Understanding for Collaborative Control," *IEEE Transactions on Systems, Man and Cybernetics, Part A* **35**(4), pp. 494-504, July 2005.

59 Dorais, G.A., et al., "Adjustable Autonomy for Human-Centered Autonomous Systems," Proceedings of the Workshop on Adjustable Autonomy Systems (IJCAI), 1999.

60 Schreckenghost, D., et al., "Human-Agent Teams for Extended Control Operations in Space," Proceedings of the 2004 AAAI Spring Symposium on Interaction, 2004.

61 Martin, C. Schreckenghost, D. Bonasso, P. Kortenkamp, D. Milam, T., and Thronesbery, C., "Distributed Collaboration Among Humans and Software Control 77 Agents," Proceeding of the 7th International Symposium on Artificial Intelligence, 2003.

62 Kortenkamp, D., "Designing An Architecture for Adjustably Autonomous Robot Teams," In PRICAI Workshop Reader, LNAI 2112 , eds. R. Kowalcyk, S. W. Lake, N., Reed, and G. Williams, Springer-Verlag, New York, 2001.

63 Fong, T., Collaborative *Control: A Robot-Centric Model for Vehicle Teleoperation.* Ph.D. Thesis, Carnegie Mellon University, 2001.

64 Murphy, R. & Rogers, E., "Cooperative Assistance for Remote Robot Supervision," Presence, 5(2), 1996.

65 Holtzblatt, H. & Jones, S., "Contextual Inquiry: A Participatory Technique for System Esign," In D. Schuler And A. Namioka (Eds.), Participatory Design: Principles and Practice. Lawrence Erlbaum, 1993.

66 Albus, J., et al., 4D/RCS: A Reference Model Architecture For Unmanned Vehicle Systems, Version 2.0, NISTIR 6910, Gaithersburg, MD, 2002.

67 Fleming, M. & Cohen, R., "A Utility-Based Theory of Initiative in Mixed-Initiative Systems," The IJCAI-01 Workshop on Autonomy, Delegation, and Control: Interacting with Autonomous Agents, 2001.

68 ASTM Standards E2521-07, *Standard Terminology for Urban Search and Rescue Robotic Operations*, ASTM International, West Conshohocken, PA, 2007.

69 Brainov, S. & Hexmoor, H., "Quantifying Relative Autonomy in Multiagent Interaction," The IJCAI-01 Workshop on Autonomy, Delegation, and Control: Interacting with Autonomous Agents, 2001.

70 Barber, K., Martin, C., Reed, N., & Kortenkamp, D., "Dimensions of Adjustable Autonomy," In Advances in Artificial Intelligence: PRICAI 2000 Workshop Reader, (eds.) R. Kowalczyk, S. W. Loke, N. Reed, and G. Williams, eds.), vol. 2112, pp. 353—361. Berlin: Springer Verlag, 2001.

71 Goodrich, M. Crandall, J.W. & Stimpson, J. L., "Neglect Tolerant Teaming: Issues and Dilemmas," Proceedings of the 2003 AAAI Spring Symposium on Human Interaction with Autonomous Systems in Complex Environments, 2003.

72 Schipani, S., An Evaluation of Operator Workload, During Partially-Autonomous Vehicle Operations, U.S. Army Research Laboratory, Aberdeen Proving Ground, Maryland, 2003.

73 Hart, S. G. and Staveland., L. E. (1988). Development of a Multi-Dimensional Workload Rating Scale: Results of Empirical and Theoretical Research, in P. A. Hancock & N. Meshkati (Eds.), Human Mental Workload. Amsterdam, The Netherlands: Elsevier.

74 Casali, J. G. and Wierwille, W. W., "A Comparison of Rating Scale, Secondary-Task, Physiological, and Primary-Task Workload Estimation Techniques in a Simulated Flight Task Emphasizing Communications Load," Human Factors, 25(6), 623-641, 1983.

75 Shingledecker, C.A., Brabtre, M.S., and Action, W.H., "Standardized Tests for the Evaluation and Classification of Workload Metrics," Proceedings of the Human Factors Society 26th Annual Meeting, 648-651, 1982.

76 Ghiselli, E. E., Campbell, J. P., and Zedeck, S., Measurement Theory for The Behavioral Sciences, San Francisco, CA: W. H. Freeeman & Co, 1981.

77 Chiles, W. D. and Alluisi, E. A., "On The Specification of Operator or Occupational Workload with Performance-Measurement Methods," Human Factors, 21(5), 515-528, 1979.

78 Gopher, D.L. and Donshin, E., Handbook of Perception and Human Performance, Volume 2 (A87-33501 14-53). New York, Wiley-Interscience, pp. 41-1 to 41-49, USAF-Navy-DARPA-supported research, 1986.

79 O'Donnell, R.D. and Eggemeier, F.T., *Handbook of Perception and Human Performance*, Volume 2 (A87-33501 14-53). New York, Wiley-Interscience, pp. 42-1 to 42-49, 1986.

80 Cameron, J.A. and Urzi, D.A., Taxonomies *of organizational behaviors: A synthesis*, CSERIAC Technical Report TR-99-002, 1999.

81 Pew, R.W. and Mavor, A.S., *Modeling Human and Organizational Behavior: Application to Military Simulation*, National Academy Press, 1998.

82 Ortony, A., Clore, G.L., and Collins, A., *The Cognitive Structure of Emotions*, Cambridge University Press, 1988.

83 Wickens, C.D., The Effects of Control Dynamics on Performance, *Handbook of Perception and Human Performance*, Volume II, John Wiley and Sons (Eds.), Sec. VII, Ch.39, 1986.

84 Fleishman, E.A., and Quaintance, M.K., *Taxonomies of Human Performance*, Academic Press Inc., New York, 1984.

85 Farina, A.J. and Wheaton, G.R., *Development of Taxonomy of Human Performance: The Task Characteristics Approach to Performance Prediction*, American Institutes for Research, Washington, DC, AIR Technical Report TR-7, 1971.

86 Schipani, S., et al., *Quantification of Cognitive Process Degradation While Mobile, Attributable to the Environmental Stressors Endurance, Vibration, and Noise*, US Army Research Laboratory, 1998.

87 Baddeley, A.D. , Attention and performance, 9. Hillsdale, NJ: Lawrence Erlbaum Associates, 1981.

88 Guinard, J.C., Landrum, G.J., and Reardon, E., Experimental Evaluation of International Standard (ISO 2631-1974) for Whole-Body Vibration Exposures, Final Report to the National Institute of Occupational Safety & Health, UDRI-TR-76-79), University of Dayton Research Institute, Dayton, Ohio, 1976.

89 Bar-Cohen, Y. and Breazeal, C., Biologically Inspired Intelligent Robots, SPIE PRESS, Bellingham, WA, 2003.

90 Barbera, Anthony et al., "Software Engineering for Intelligent Control Systems" Special Issue of Software Engineering for Knowledge-Intensive Systems, KI Journal, Volume 3, Issue 4.

91 Jones, J. and Ragon, M., "Development of Autonomy Levels Through Functional Decomposition and Allocation," Proceedings of American Helicopter Society Forum 2007, Virginia Beach, VA

92 Seels, B. and Glasgow, Z., *Exercises in Instructional Design*, Columbus OH: Merrill Publishing Company, 1990.

93 Harrow, A.J., *A Taxonomy of The Psychomotor Domain*, New York: David Mckay Co., 1972.

94 Krathwohl, D.R., Bloom, B.S., and Masia, B.B., *Taxonomy of Educational Objectives: Handbook II: Affective Domain*, New York: David Mckay Co., 1964.

95 Miller, G.A., "The Magical Number Seven, Plus or Minus Two: Some Limits on Our Capacity for Processing Information," The Psychological Review, Vol. 63, Pp. 81-97, 1956.

96 Cohen, D., "Analysis of Workload Predictions Generated by Multiple Resource Theory," Aviation Space and Environmental Medicine, 67(2), Feb., Pp. 139-145, 1996.

97 Klapp, S.T and Netick, A., "Multiple Resources for Processing and Storage in Short-Term Memory," Human Factors, 30(5), pp. 617-632, 1988.

98 Wickens, C.D., Gordon, S.E; Liu, Y., An Introduction to Human Factors Engineering. Addison-Wesley, ISBN: 0321012291, 1998.

99 Wickens, C.D., *Multiple Resources and Performance Prediction, Theoretical Issues in Ergonomics Science*, 3(2), pp. 150-177, 2002.

100 Barbera, A., et al., "How Task Analysis Can Be Used to Derive and Organize the Knowledge For the Control of Autonomous Vehicles," AAAI Symposium, 2004.

101 Barbera, A., et al., "How Task Analysis Can Be Used to Derive and Organize the Knowledge For the Control of Autonomous Vehicles," (expanded version) Robotics and Autonomous Systems, Volume 99, Issues 1 – 2.

102 Albus, J.S., "Task Decomposition," Proceedings of the 8th IEEE International Symposium on Intelligent Control, Chicago, IL, August 25-27, 1993.

103 Huang, H.M. and Quintero, R., "Task Decomposition Methodology for the Design of a Coal Mining Automation Hierarchical Real-Time Control System," Proceedings of the 5th IEEE International Symposium on Intelligent Control, Philadelphia, PA, September 5-7, 1990.

104 Ryan, M.E., The Tokaimura Nuclear Accident: A Tragedy of Human Errors. Journal of College Science Teaching, Vol. 31(1) P42-48 September, 2001.

105 Miller, G.A., "The Magical Number Seven, Plus or Minus Two: Some Limits on Our Capacity for Processing Information," The Psychological Review, Vol. 63, Pp. 81-97, 1956.

106 Cohen, D., "Analysis of Workload Predictions Generated by Multiple Resource Theory," Aviation Space and Environmental Medicine, 67(2), Feb., Pp. 139-145, 1996.

107 Klapp, S.T & Netick, A., "Multiple Resources for Processing and Storage in Short-Term Memory," Human Factors, 30(5), pp. 617-632, 1988.

108 Wickens, C.D., Gordon, S.E; Liu, Y., An Introduction to Human Factors Engineering, Addison-Wesley, ISBN: 0321012291, 1998.

109 Wickens, C.D., Multiple Resources and Performance Prediction, Theoretical Issues in Ergonomics Science, 3(2), pp. 150-177, 2002.

110 Jacoff, A., Weiss, B, Messina, E., "Evolution of a Performance Metric for Urban Search and Rescue Robots (2003)," Proceedings of the 2003 Performance Metrics for Intelligent Systems (PerMIS) Workshop, NIST Special Publication 1014, Gaithersburg, MD, August 16 - 18, 2003.

111 Messina, E. and Jacoff, A., "Performance Standards for Urban Search and Rescue Robots," Proceedings of the SPIE Defense and Security Symposium, Orlando, FL, April 17-21, 2006.

112 Process/Industrial Instruments and Control Handbook, McGraw-Hill Handbooks Series, McGraw-Hill Professional Publishing, NY, NY 1999.

113 Crick, M., et al., Emergency Management in the Early Phase, Emergency Preparedness and Response Section, Department of Nuclear Safety and Security, International Atomic Energy Agency, A-1400 Vienna, Austria, 2004.

114 DTIC Accession Number AD0645054: Comparison of Merited Grade and Skill Level Ratings of Airman Jobs, http://stinet.dtic.mil/oai/oai?&verb=getRecord&metadataPrefix=html&identifier=AD0645054, Defense Technology Information Center, Fort Belvoir, VA.

115 http://www.trainingfinder.org/competencies/list_levels.htm.

116 http://www.us-army-info.com/pages/mos/skills.html.